An Illustrated Guide
to London 1800

The Monument and St Magnus Church

An Illustrated Guide to London 1800

MARY CATHCART BORER

St. Martin's Press   New York

Library of Congress Cataloging-in-Publication Data
Borer, Mary Irene Cathcart.
An illustrated guide to London, 1800 / Mary Cathcart Borer.
    p.   cm.
ISBN 0-312-02778-8
    1. London (England—Description—To 1800—Guide-books., 2. London
(England)—History—1800–1950.   3. Historic sites—England—London—
Guide-books.   I. Title
DA679.B73   1988
914.21′04858—dc19   88-39717
                                                                      CIP

First published in Great Britain by Robert Hale Limited
First U.S. Edition

Photoset in Palatino by
Rowland Phototypesetting Limited, Bury St Edmunds, Suffolk
Printed in Great Britain by St Edmundsbury Press Limited,
Bury St Edmunds, Suffolk
Bound by WBC Limited

Contents

Illustrations

PICTURE CREDITS

The Guildhall Library: 1, 5, 8, 22, 24, 25, 27, 28, 29, 30, 36, 37, 40, 45, 52, 56, 61, 62, 64, 88, 90. Mary Evans Picture Library: 7, 32, 47, 58, 72, 74, 75, 87.

Acknowledgements

I should like to thank Cassell & Company for permission to use some of the illustrations from the six volumes of their *Old and New London*, published in 1888–93; R. J. W. Gieves, Vice-Chairman of Gieves & Hawkes, for the information he has given me of the two firms before their amalgamation: and Jonathan Cape Limited, for permission to quote from *Sophie in London – 1786*, the diary and letters of Sophie v. la Roche, translated from the German by Clare Williams and published in 1933.

M.C.B.

Preface

This is a picture of the City of London in 1800. The British Empire was newly established and waiting to be explored, developed and populated.

All through the previous century men had been experimenting in the devising of new mechanical and power-driven machinery, and after many disappointments and failures their work was at last succeeding. It was to bring about the Industrial Revolution. Yet in 1800 few Londoners realized the changes which, within the next few years, were to affect their lives so profoundly.

I have written the book in the first person, in order to guide the reader around the city as a visitor.

1. Introduction to London

London's story is one of steady development through nearly 1,700 years, from a small Roman encampment to the largest and most important city in the world. Today, in the year 1800, it means two things: the square mile of the ancient city, with its special privilege of self-government, and its ever-increasing surroundings, which now stretch into Middlesex, Surrey and Kent.

When the Romans invaded Britain, Celtic tribes who had settled there some centuries earlier were already trading tin, silver, gold, iron, corn, cattle and wool with Europe. The Roman army landed on the Kent coast and reached the north bank of the Thames by a hastily built bridge of rafts, and there they paused to await reinforcements. They quickly realized the strategic advantage of this site, for it was almost at the limit of tidal waters, which made for the easier handling of heavily laden boats. It was the first rising ground – today known as Cornhill – above the malarial Essex marshes. It could be easily reached by trading vessels from Europe, yet was far enough inland to be safe from marauding raiders. It lay on a river which reached far into the heart of the country.

During the 400 years of their occupation, the Romans improved the port facilities, building quays along the waterfront and river walls to hold back the floodwaters. When the barbarian Picts from Scotland and the Celtic Scots from Ireland began their incursions into Britain, the Romans built a defensive wall round Londinium from just east of the Walbrook in a wide arc reaching Ludgate in the west and then curving down to the river again, a stretch of more than 2½ miles. Outside the wall there was little building as yet, except round the southern bridgehead (Southwark).

In the fourth century, when the Angles and Saxons from Europe invaded the south-east of Britain, Londinium was protected by its wall, but when Rome herself was attacked by nomadic Mongols from central Asia, and recalled her legions to try to defend her crumbling empire, her rule in Britain was at an end. A few years later Rome was captured and the great days of the Empire were over.

An illustrated map of the cities of London and Westminster and the borough of Southwark in 1799

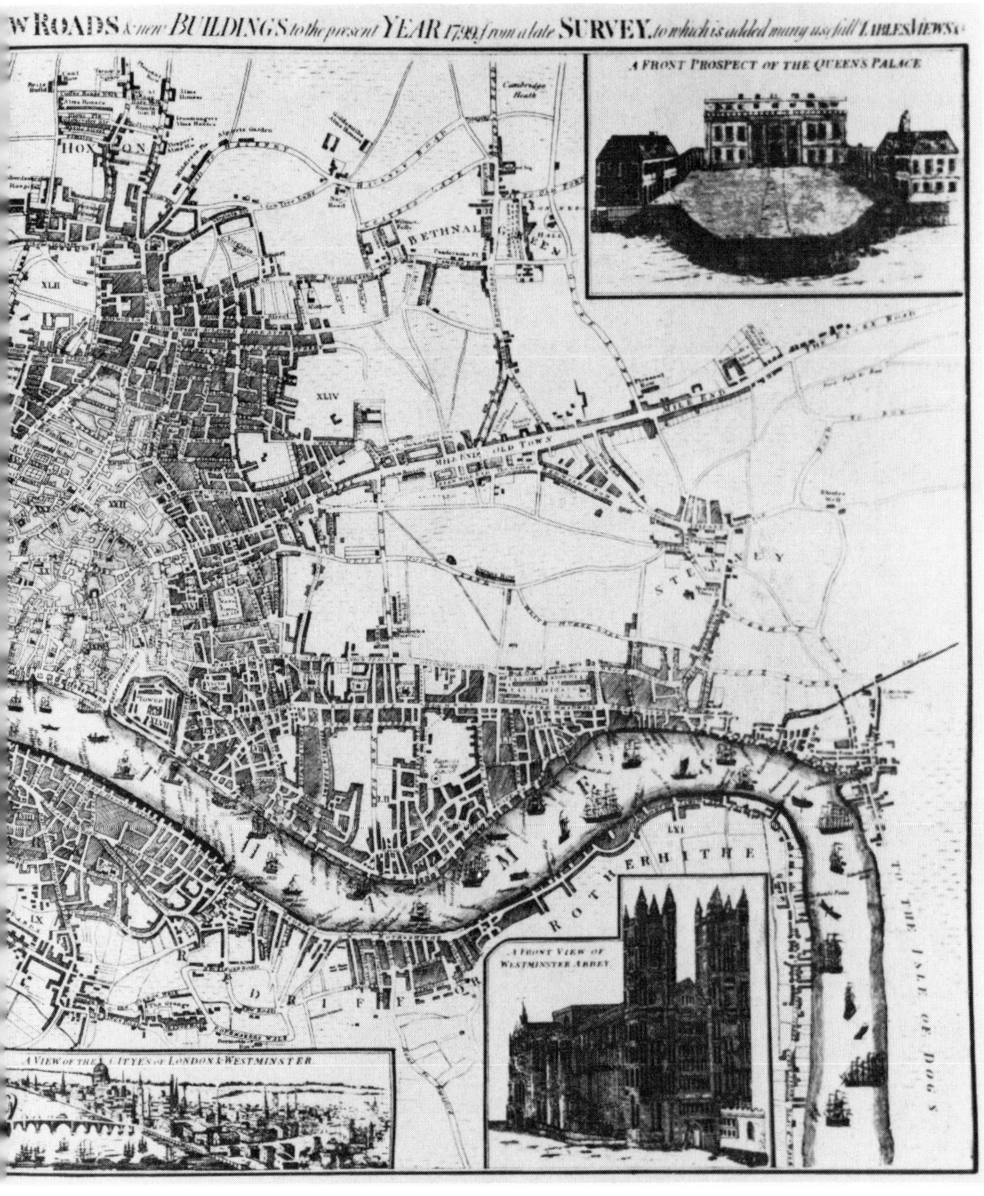

A FRONT PROSPECT OF THE QUEEN'S PALACE

HOXTON

BETHNAL GREEN

Cambridge Heath

XLII

XLIV

MILE END OLD TOWN

XXII

STEPNEY

ROTHERHITHE

To THE ISLE OF DOGS

A FRONT VIEW OF WESTMINSTER ABBEY

A VIEW OF THE CITYES OF LONDON & WESTMINSTER

R
D
RIFF

There was no centralized government left in Britain, the foreign trade on which London had thrived disappeared, and for the next fifty years the city was almost deserted. Now Britain became England, and there emerged from the confusion and bloodshed four individual kingdoms, south of Hadrian's Wall.

Eventually European traders appeared at London's deserted wharves with cargoes of pottery, glass and wine to offer in exchange for English wool and metals. A few Saxons, the first London merchants, moved into the empty city, and slowly a small foreign trade with the Continent was re-established. The English renovated the quays and river walls and set about building a new city within the old Roman walls.

A Roman abbot, Augustine, and his band of monks arrived in 597 and began the conversion of the English to Christianity, King Ethelbert of Kent building the little cathedral of St Paul in the heart of the city.

In the ninth century England was invaded yet again, when the Danish and Norwegian Vikings sailed up the Thames to overrun the greater part of the country, but Alfred, King of Wessex, succeeded in turning them out of London, which he occupied in 886, establishing his son-in-law Ethelred as lord of the City.

The Danish Vikings began gradually to assimilate the culture and religion of the people whose land they had invaded, and they proved excellent traders. Now from London's quays went wool, corn and animal skins, and in return came wine, fish and pottery from Rouen, timber and pitch from Scandinavia; even Far Eastern produce – pepper and spices, ivory and silks and rich brocades – eventually reached London, having come by Arab dhows across the Indian Ocean to Arabia, by camel caravans over the desert to the ports of the Levant, and thence from Venice across Germany and the Netherlands to Antwerp and the Thames.

At the end of the tenth century, there was another invasion of Danish Vikings, and the Danish Canute succeeded in welding the four English provinces into one kingdom, over which he reigned as king. From the fusion of conflicting temperaments and ancestries, people sank their differences and began to identify themselves with the soil of England, and the beginnings of a national unity emerged, with London as the capital city.

London thrived, and its tolls, collected by the port-reeve, swelled the King's treasury. The City became cosmopolitan. On its wharves wine merchants from Rouen traded and settled in the Vintry. Cloth merchants from Flanders and Cologne lived round Dowgate, where the Walbrook joins the Thames. Round the market-place of East Cheap lived the goldsmiths from Ghent and Ponthieu. The City became an enclosed world ruled by its merchants. It was a state within a state, a self-governing community of freemen who owned land and shared the responsibility of governing their city.

The citizens of London acquired the power to give their approval or disapproval at the election of a king, who was chosen from the most promising members of the royal family.

It was the Londoners who persuaded Edward the Confessor to retire to Westminster and allow his brother-in-law Harold to reign as Under-King. (At Westminster, Edward built a small wooden palace and began the rebuilding of the little seventh-century minster dedicated to St Peter.) On Edward's death, in 1066, Harold was proclaimed King, but Duke William of Normandy insisted that Edward had named him his heir and landed in England only a few months later. Harold was killed in the first battle, and William advanced on London.

After much negotiation, London accepted the Norman as the new ruler but insisted that he respect the City's special privilege of self-government. Hoping to borrow money from the City, William did not disagree but, well aware of London's power, was prepared to use force at any sign of trouble and ordered the building of the massive White Tower, the beginning of the Tower of London, just outside the eastern wall of the City.

Wool was now the country's most valuable export. London's central market was Cheapside, where wares were displayed in booths and sheds; and from Cheapside ran the streets where particular commodities were offered: Poultry, Honey, Iron, Milk and Wood Street to the north, Money-Changing, Fish, Soap, Candles and Bread Street to the south, while along the river were the great breweries.

The City was now divided into small administrative districts – by the early part of the twelfth century there were twenty-four, each ward being named after the alderman at the head of its administration. Some of the wards were now stretching outside the City wall, and by 1222 the City had reached its present boundary, covering an approximate square mile. During these years the hundred or more little City churches were built, most of them established by wealthy citizens, who maintained them and supported a priest from their own donations.

Henry II established Westminster as his Court, London as the meeting-place of his councils. It therefore became necessary for the lords and peers of the realm to maintain households in the

Bow church, Cheapside. Home of the original Bow bells

City or its suburbs, close to the source of power and influence.

Work on the first stone bridge over the Thames was begun in 1176, financed largely by a new tax on wool. In the middle was built a two-storey chapel dedicated to St Thomas Becket. London traders, seeing the importance of the site, quickly established themselves there, and soon the bridge was almost completely lined with houses and shops, built up against the parapets, the roadway passing through the centre.

When Richard I exacted money from London for his crusade, in 1189, the City received in return its first legal grant towards self-government. The freemen from each ward now elected an alderman to sit on their governing council, and from these aldermen they also elected each year a sheriff. A few years later there is the mention of a mayor of London, his title meaning 'the chief of the community'. From Richard's successor, King John, the City demanded that their mayor be elected annually, and he granted them a charter which allowed this, provided the candidate's name be submitted for his approval at the time of the election. The mayor's procession therefore had to travel each year up the river to Westminster, to give the oath of loyalty to the tribunal of the Exchequer. Today the ritual continues, and they return to the Fleet canal, where they land and mount their horses, to ride in procession to the Guildhall for their feast. From the outset the mayor of London was addressed as 'Your Worship', but only intermittently was he called 'the Lord Mayor', and the title was not used regularly until 1545.

Henry III rebuilt most of Westminster Abbey, borrowing or demanding money from the Jews, whom William the Conqueror had introduced to finance his large building programme, but by the middle of the thirteenth century the Lombards had arrived in London, establishing themselves in Lombard Street and acting as bankers and pawnbrokers. Soon they were lending money to the government, taking a mortgage on customs dues as surety. The Jews had long been resented because of the high interest they charged on their loans, and now they soon found themselves out of business. In the end, Edward I forbade them to practise usury on pain of death, and in 1290 some 15,000 were expelled from the country.

The first friars had arrived in London by this time – the black-robed friars of St Dominic establishing themselves in Holborn, the grey friars of St Francis in Newgate, and the white friars of the Carmelite order on the riverside, near the church of the Knights Templars.

German merchants also came to London and settled in their guild house on the river at Dowgate. They represented the Hanseatic League of north German trading towns, and their settlement was called the Steelyard – a corruption of *Stapelhof*, meaning a courtyard where samples of merchandise are stored and displayed. They provided transport for London's overseas trade, at a time when the city had not sufficient for its needs, and also provided useful loans to the Crown.

In 1273 the Common Council of the City of London was formed, a group of twenty-five men, elected by the community, to consult with the mayor, the sheriffs and the aldermen on City affairs.

The ancient craft guilds, which men practising the same crafts had established for their mutual protection, were now transformed into companies of crafts under the leadership of a master. And now a new rank was established amongst them – the Livery men. These were the upper ranks of the free craftsmen who, alone in the company, were entitled to wear the distinctive dress, and only from them were members of the governing body chosen. The election of the mayor, sheriffs and other officers has remained in the hands of the livery companies ever since.

The wool trade was changing. Edward III invited Flemish weavers to London to teach their craft, and by the end of the fourteenth century the Company of Staplers had been established, which had a partial monopoly of the export of wool. Despite the heavy taxes imposed by the King, these merchants, operating between London and Calais and with close connexions with the Cotswolds, from where the best wool came, grew wealthy and can be regarded as the first English capitalists. Then the King forbade the import of foreign cloth. The manufacture of cloth became a rural industry throughout England, bringing prosperity to the collecting towns and even more wealth to London, from which it was exported.

This increasing volume of business created great differences of wealth between the merchant employing many people and the old master craftsman who employed only a few journeymen and apprentices, thereby bringing about a social gulf between master and employee. In time the old craft guilds were abolished by Act of Parliament and their estates bought in by the Livery Companies.

For the next 300 years the Livery Companies wielded great power in the City and shaped its history. Only the Merchant Taylors and the Goldsmiths had halls before 1400, but during the next century twenty-six more were built.

The City's medieval splendour had not yet decayed. The

Loaded wagons rattle down St Martin's Lane

priories, abbeys and convents, set in their carefully tended gardens, the cathedral of St Paul and the beautiful conventual churches, the little parish churches with their chantries and grave-yards, still covered a quarter of the area within the boundaries of the City, while along the river front, between the quays and warehouses, in the narrow streets running up from the waterside to Watling Street, along the Strand leading to Westminster and throughout the City were the London mansions of the noblemen.

However, the Reformation wrought devastating changes in the City. Many of the churches and monastic buildings were destroyed. On the site of a Cistercian abbey close to the Tower of London, and the convent of St Clare nearby, cottages were built for dock labourers. The priory of Holy Trinity in Lombard Street came down, the stones and monuments sold for building material. St Mary's Spital, by the Bishop's Gate, was demolished, and new houses were built on the ground. The Church of the Knights Hospitallers was blown up with gunpowder.

The Royal Dockyard, Deptford

Over the gardens spread crowded courtyards and little twisting lanes, lined with houses for artisans and craftsmen, and eastwards from the Tower, says the topographer Stow, grew 'a continual street of filthy straight passages, with alleys of small tenements or cottages builded, inhabited by sailors' victuallers, along the River Thames, almost to Radcliffe'.

At the beginning of the sixteenth century the population of London, including its suburbs and the little villages of Charing and Westminster, was approaching 100,000; by the end of the century it had nearly doubled and was still increasing.

Living in Lombard Street during the 1550s was Sir Thomas Gresham, a financier and merchant who initiated the building of an exchange, similar to those of Venice and Antwerp, where merchandise could be properly displayed. A space was cleared on Cornhill, near the Stocks market, and here rose Gresham's great bourse, opened by Queen Elizabeth I in 1570 and named by her 'the Royal Exchange'. The impetus to the trade of London was tremendous, and London's business boomed.

After the Queen had expelled the foreign Steelyard merchants, in 1579, London financed her own trading companies of merchant adventurers to send goods to Russia, Prussia, the Baltic, Turkey and the Levant. At the same time citizens seized the opportunity provided by new sea routes to begin trading with Persia and India by way of the Cape, and in 1600 Queen Elizabeth granted a charter to the largest of London's trading companies – the East India Company.

While East India Company ships plied between London and Madras, Bombay and Bengal, with cargoes of silk and spices, and saltpetre for gunpowder, the first American colonies, using imported Negro labour, were growing valuable crops of cotton, tobacco and cane sugar, which they exported to England. London's fortunes prospered, and to accommodate the stores of wealth which merchants were accumulating, the goldsmiths of Lombard Street opened the first banking houses, depositing their cash in the Exchequer.

At the accession of Charles II in 1660, the population of the country was about 5½ million, of which London accounted for nearly half a million. The Netherlands were now England's main trade rival, and within four years of Charles II's accession war had broken out with the Dutch. When the King borrowed £1,300,000 from the Exchequer to pursue the war, the City decided that the time was ripe for a 'Bank of England', where its money would be safely under its own control, but before it could materialize,

*Horwood's plan of 1792–99 showing the site of the Bank of England,
now under construction, and, to the north, Moorfields and Bethlem
Hospital*

London was stricken by the two devastating disasters of the Plague in 1665 and the Great Fire in 1666.

In the City alone, although two-thirds of the population moved away during the Plague, nearly half of those who remained – some 70,000 – perished. After the Great Fire, there remained little of the City but charred ruins: 436 acres, more than 300 of them within the walls, had been destroyed, including 13,200 houses, the halls of forty-four of the Companies, and eighty-nine parish churches, as well as St Paul's Cathedral, the Royal Exchange, the Customs House, part of the Guildhall and four of the City gates.

The most immediate need was to house the homeless. Some contrived small sheds on the smouldering ruins of their former homes. Others moved into the suburbs, setting up their shops in the Strand or moving down to Wapping and Deptford. When more still began to move even farther afield, the Corporation of London realized the danger of this exodus. London had to be rebuilt as quickly as possible, and its population, with all its skills, trading connexions and accumulated wealth must be held together, or the whole organization might disintegrate.

The Rebuilding Act was passed in 1667, and to enable rebuilding to begin, the City was granted a levy of a shilling a ton on coal coming into London for the next ten years, and this was later raised to 3 shillings a ton. Wren designed a series of wide streets running from a central point, but legal difficulties arose from the various ownerships of the ground, and he was not able to accomplish all he had visualized. His new brick houses were plain, square and comfortable, with sashed windows and hipped roofs. Three sizes were allowed – four, three or two storeys, all with a cellar and garret.

The rebuilding of the churches began in 1670 and went on for the next thirty years – the first stone of the new St Paul's was laid in 1675. The City spread its own building programme over the next seven years, beginning with the Guildhall and Sessions House, Royal Exchange and Customs House. But in 1672, by which time many of the halls of the Livery Companies had been rebuilt, King Charles was faced with bankruptcy, and Sir Thomas Clifford proposed that, 'As the King must have money to carry on the war with Holland, in which his honour is engaged, he knew of no other means at present than shutting up of the Exchequer.' It confirmed the goldsmiths' worst fears, for it meant that the King had appropriated their money, which he intended to treat as a loan at six per cent. For a time they had no money available to make payments to customers, and many bankers and their clients were financially ruined.

Yet the work of rebuilding went on, and by 1676 a vastly improved City had come into existence. Drains and sewers had been laid, and water from the New River Company or the rival London Bridge waterworks was already being supplied to many of the neat, red-brick dwellings. In the heart of the City, the new Royal Exchange was now the focal point of the widened Poultry, Cornhill and Lombard Street, as well as the new Princes Street. Goldsmiths, bankers and important merchants took houses in this area, together with an increasing number of Jews, who had been allowed back into England by Oliver Cromwell.

With the Exchequer so vulnerable, the City knew that the time had now come for the formation of the long-needed Bank of England, and it was eventually established by William Paterson in 1691. At this time the Crown debt was £2 million, contracted during the long European war, and it was still rising. The problem that confronted Paterson and his colleagues was how to collect sufficient capital to fund the Bank, for a loan of £1.2 million was urgently needed.

Court of the Bank of England

An appeal for subscriptions was launched and to the surprise of many, the whole sum was forthcoming within ten days. Those who subscribed £500 or more became members of the company known as 'The Governors and Company of the Bank of England' and elected a governor, a deputy governor and twenty-four directors. Operating at first from the Grocers' Hall in the Poultry, the bank lent this money to the Crown in return for an annual payment of £100,000, which was raised by 'Rates and duties upon tonnage of ships and vessels and upon beer, ale and other liquors'. Thus it was England's supremacy on the high seas which enabled the City to maintain its position.

Now, in the year 1800, London handles more than eighty per cent of the country's imports and seventy per cent of her exports, which include coal and iron. Coal production has doubled since the 6 million tons which was produced thirty years ago, and today iron production is up to 250,000 tons a year, which has given Britain the lead in the world metal trade, for most of the tin and copper in use throughout the world still comes from Cornwall, and large quantities of lead are mined in the Pennines. The Pool of London grows busier every year, with merchant vessels arriving from every country in Europe. The traffic now outstrips the port facilities, so that many ships have to ride at anchor in the fairway. The London docks are being rebuilt: this year the West India Dock has been opened, and plans are being made for the construction of two more docks, to be called the East India and Surrey Commercial docks. Quays and wharves are being enlarged and more warehouses have been built to house the unloaded goods until such time as they can be marketed, the East India Dock Company building many in Cutler Street.

Customs inspection is an increasing problem, for although the docks are so close to the City, living on the river banks is the most disreputable collection of pirates, night plunderers, mudlarks (street arabs) and receivers of all kinds, who seem to evade the most careful watch. De Saussure, a Swiss visitor to London in recent years who recorded his impressions, wrote of the strict customs search. 'The officers', he said, 'are extraordinarily clever at discovering anything contraband, a share going into their own pockets.' They noticed that the breeches of one of his travelling companions, a French refugee captain, were rather bulky in the seat and found a packet of Flanders lace hidden there. They then turned their attention to the captain's mother and sister, and 'being impudent enough to search beneath the ladies' petticoats, found several more packets of lace'.

'The hall on the first floor of the Customs House,' he continued, 'was so crowded with merchants, captains of vessels and other applicants that you have difficulty in making your way in', and the bargemen '. . . use singular and even quite extraordinary terms, and generally very coarse and dirty ones, and I cannot explain them to you'.

Like other European countries, Britain imports slave labour from Africa for New World colonies, and within recent years there has been an intensification of the trade. When planters retire, they often bring slaves back to Britain as personal servants, and it is highly fashionable to have a Negro boy on the household staff, usually acting as a page. When ladies go shopping, they take him with them, to carry their purchases, and if, as sometimes happens, a slave runs away, advertisements and rewards for his recovery are advertised in the newspapers. There is a trade in these slaves in London – during the 1750s some 20,000 were bought and sold at the Royal Exchange, each one branded and wearing a padlocked collar engraved with the name or coat of arms of his owner.

The Quakers of Pennsylvania published their protest against slavery more than a hundred years ago, and with the passing years an increasing number of people have expressed their horror at the cruelty of the trade, but it was not until a few years ago that William Wilberforce, with information supplied by John Newton, began his work for their liberation. In 1787 an Anti-Slavery Committee was formed in London, under the presidency of Granville Sharp, and two years later the Committee bought land in Sierra Leone for the settlement of freed American Negroes. The little colony, as yet only 400 strong, has been established in Freetown.

The founding of the London Missionary Society five years ago, and the Colonial Missionary Society only last year, has strengthened the anti-slavery movement. The northern states of America no longer buy slaves. The French Revolutionary Committee has made the trade illegal, and few people doubt that within the next few years it will also become illegal in Britain.

During the past century Britain has been almost constantly at war with France, in the course acquiring the island of Minorca and the strategic stronghold of Gibraltar (affording control of entrance to the Mediterranean for merchant ships). Over the past forty years Britain has also laid the foundations of an empire in India, wrested Canada from the French and claimed possession of lands discovered by Captain Cook, in his travels from 1768 to 1771: Australia, New Zealand and many of the islands of Polynesia – compensation indeed for the loss of the American colonies in 1776.

William Wilberforce, social reformer

But now Britain's long struggle with France is intensifying. In 1789 the people of France began their Revolution, which increases every year in violence and cruelty. In 1793 they declared war on Britain. Napoleon Bonaparte is fast rising to power in France and is said to be preparing an invasion force. Many people in the southern and south-eastern coastal towns have already packed their possessions and come to London, to stay with relations or friends. Everywhere there are wild rumours and false alarms of invasion. So far it has not happened, but every day the danger seems nearer.

Throughout this long war Britain has maintained her exports, although there have been periods of blockade when trade has been seriously interrupted, causing unemployment and great distress in some industrial areas. The nation's supply of foreign wheat has now been cut off, and prices have more than doubled from the 50 shillings a quarter of seven years ago. Yet, while the poor suffer hardship, the middle and upper classes have been little affected by the war, while the City has grown wealthier than ever.

The Swiss traveller de Saussure, who died last year, considered that the British were 'esteemed for their wealth more than anything else' and that, 'Commerce was not looked down upon as being derogatory, as it is in France and Germany. Here men of good family and even of rank become merchants without losing caste.' All that is changing: members of the professions and the academics now regard themselves as socially superior to those in commerce.

Merchants come from humbler origins now, often having risen from ordinary retail tradesmen, but the Londoner's tradition of absolute integrity in his business dealings and the proud assertion that his word is his bond remain unsullied. It is a tradition which has persisted ever since the City was established, more than a thousand years ago, for many pagan Roman Londoners were worshippers of Mithras, a god not only of fertility and victory in battle but of truth and the inviolability of the pledged word.

This year bakers have been forbidden to sell bread until it has been out of the oven for twenty-four hours, and with the French intensifying their attacks on British imports of wheat, the King has just issued a proclamation exhorting all his people to use the utmost economy in bread and flour.

2. Exploring London

In this year of Our Lord 1800, the population of England and Wales is between 8 and 9 millions, but London, now twelve times the size of any other city in the kingdom, is still spreading, so that today a million people are regarded as Londoners, although only some 134,000 live within the square mile of the City's boundaries.

London stretches for four miles from east to west, and for two miles from north to south. It includes on the south side of the river the villages of Lambeth, Newington, Camberwell, Putney, Clapham, Wandsworth, Rotherhithe, Streatham, Battersea, Bermondsey and Richmond, and on the north side, Kensington, Chelsea, Fulham, Hammersmith, Chiswick, Ealing, Edmonton, Tottenham, Enfield, Harrow, Twickenham, Staines and Uxbridge.

These suburban villages are all regarded as part of London now, though their administration, with the exception of Lambeth, is still in the hands of the counties in which they have developed, but it has been suggested that one day the City and its suburbs will be created a county on their own, with the one administration for all their inhabitants.

The main thoroughfares of London north of the Thames run roughly parallel with the river. The mile-long stretch of Oxford Street runs due east to Holborn. To the south is Piccadilly, and south again the Strand, running east to Fleet Street, which reaches Ludgate Hill. At the top of the hill, skirting St Paul's Cathedral to the north, the way eastwards continues as Cheapside, Poultry, Cornhill, Leadenhall Street and Whitechapel High Street to the fields and sparsely populated Mile End New Town, with the rural Bethnal Green to the north and Stepney to the south.

Despite all the new building of recent years, there are still islands of squalor in London. In Old Westminster and Tothill Fields, which have now joined up with Chelsea, there are evil little streets and alleys – Cabbage Lane, Rogue's Acre, Dirty Lane, Long Ditch, Pickpocket Alley and Bandy Leg Walk, while the wide space between Charing Cross and the end of the Mall, below the royal stables, is a rookery of ramshackle buildings and hovels, murky

Bowle's one-sheet plan of London, 1800

alleys and dingy courts. They are strange, ugly places but with exotic names such as Caribee Islands and the Bermudas, and in the middle is Porridge Island, well known for its dubious cooking. This patch of desolation, onto which James Gibbs' beautiful church of St Martin-in-the-Fields faces, is no better than the rookeries of St Giles just to the north.

The eastern spread of London is sadly different from the Mayfair development. Partly because of the manner of land tenure, which has enabled copyhold tenants to let on short leases, Stepney, Spitalfields, Ratcliffe, Limehouse, Wapping, St George's in the East, Mile End and Bethnal Green have filled out in a straggling, haphazard way, while along the south bank of the river are the tanneries of Bermondsey and the timberyards of Lambeth.

J. W. Archenholtz, a recent German visitor to London, was surprised at the uneven development of the capital: 'The east end,' he said, 'especially along the shores of the Thames, consists of old houses, the streets are narrow, dark and ill-paved. . . . The contrast between this and the west end is astonishing: the houses here are mostly new and elegant; the squares are superb, the streets are straight and open. . . .'

Kensington Palace, in the fields of the most westerly part of the city, is a good spot from which to begin an exploration of London. From the palace runs a muddy track leading eastwards to the little stone bridge – the Knights' Bridge – over the Walbrook stream, which flows across the road from Hyde Park to the village of Knightsbridge, with its scattered cottages and maypole on the green. People complain bitterly about the condition of this road, and there is now another hazard: on your right you will pass a number of taverns, many of which have a bad reputation, for their keepers are almost certainly in league with the highwaymen and footpads (highwaymen on foot) who lurk here after dark. Only a few months ago the *Morning Chronicle* reported that a party of light horse infantry had been ordered to patrol the road every night, and people who wish to make the journey on foot are urged to join a band of pedestrians large enough for their mutual protection, beginning their journeys at known intervals, 'of which a bell gives due warning'.

At the end of Knightsbridge is St George's Hospital, which was established in Lanesborough House after the death of Lord Lanesborough in 1733, but it has been much enlarged since then and additional wings have been built. Although it relies mainly on voluntary subscriptions, it is estimated that it has treated 150,000 patients. Just beyond the hospital is Tattersalls, the auction market for horses, which attracts buyers from all over Europe, and away to the south and the south-west are the Five Fields, leading down to Chelsea and the river.

Opposite St George's Hospital are the tollgate of Hyde Park and the red-brick Apsley House, residence of Lord Apsley, the Lord Chancellor. Northwards, along the eastern border of his garden, runs Park Lane, which until a few years ago was a desolate track known merely as 'the lane leading to Tyburn', where public hangings regularly took place.

To the east of St George's is the walled garden of one of London's royal residences, the house built by the Duke of Buckingham which in 1762 King George III bought for his Queen and their growing family. It was intended to be called 'The Queen's House', but now, despite many extensions, it is still called 'Buckingham Palace' by Londoners. It lies to the south of St James's Palace, which developed from a 'shooting box' which Henry VIII built, enclosing neighbouring fields to form the present St James's Park and the Green Park.

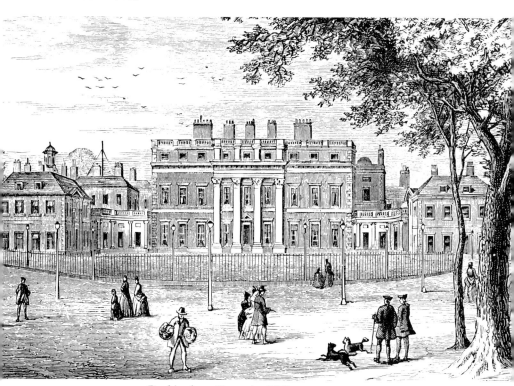

Buckingham House in 1775

33

Henry VIII's chief minister, Cardinal Wolsey, lived farther east, at York Place, halfway between Charing and the crumbling old palace of Westminster, and after the Cardinal's fall from grace the King took possession, re-naming it Whitehall Palace and adding many new buildings, as well as tennis courts and bowling greens, a cockpit and a tiltyard, so that, with the large gardens to the south, the palace precincts stretched along the riverside for half a mile. The palace was approached from the north by Holbein's gateway and from the south by the King's Gate, which gave onto the narrow King Street, leading to Westminster Abbey and the old palace.

Most of Whitehall Palace was destroyed by fire in 1619, and James I commissioned Inigo Jones to plan a new building. He designed the banqueting hall, which still stands, but the rest of the palace was never built – the Civil War turned royal attention to other matters.

Returning to St George's Hospital, we see the road called Piccadilly stretching away eastward, while to the north is Park Lane, which ends at the point where the Tyburn gallows used to be. Then from Tyburn, going east, parallel with Piccadilly, is the mile-long stretch of the Tyburn road which is now called Oxford Street.

North of Oxford Street are the Marylebone Gardens, Wigmore Lane and the green fields of the open countryside, but from the south side of Oxford Street, stretching down to Piccadilly, is the new and exclusive Mayfair, built on the fields and farmlands watered by the little Tyburn stream. The principal squares of Mayfair are Grosvenor Square, first appearing in the rate books in 1725, and Berkeley Square, which was built in the 1740s and 1750s, while Golden Square is in the north-east, rather hidden away and once described as 'not exactly in anybody's way, to or from anywhere'. Hanover Square, the oldest of the squares, built between 1716 and 1720, is farther east, behind the south side of Oxford Street, and off the north side, directly opposite, is Cavendish Square.

As early as 1720 plans were discussed for moving the Tyburn gallows to some other spot, possibly Kingsland, to save the residents of Hanover Square and the surrounding new streets from the annoyance of the passing of the death cart down Oxford Street every six weeks, with the accompanying crowds of rowdy, noisy sightseers. But it was not until 1783 that the gallows, after standing at Tyburn for 500 years, were removed to Newgate prison, so that during most of the past century the aristocratic residents of Hanover Square have turned their backs on Oxford Street, the entrance to the square, by way of the short, tree-lined and neatly paved Lady Holles Street, barred at its northern end by posts and rails.

Now the gallows are gone. Oxford Street has developed quickly, and today it is lined with shops, established mainly to supply the needs of fashionable Mayfair. A German visitor has recently said that, 'This street alone contains as many lamps as the whole of Paris, so that the scene, with shops open till ten and brightly lit, deceived the Prince of Monaco into believing all this brilliance was in his honour.'

The first mansions have been built in Park Lane, and now that Edward Shepherd's market and the noisy fair he was licensed to hold each year during the first fortnight in May have been discontinued, the building of the rest of Mayfair has proceeded steadily.

The new houses in Grosvenor Square have quickly become the focus of grandeur, elegance, fashion, taste and hospitality. However, to reach their parish church of St George, Hanover Square, the residents had to make their way – or be carried in their sedans – through the Berkeley Wood, which slopes down to the Tyburn brook. This was not only a troublesome journey in the dark days of winter but also a highly dangerous one, for the wood is a notorious haunt of footpads.

In 1730, at the time South Audley Street was built, Sir Richard Grosvenor arranged for the building of the Grosvenor Chapel. It is sited to face straight down the short length of Aldford Street onto Park Lane and Hyde Park and is designed for a congregation of some 1,200.

With the end of the fair, more houses were built along the western part of Piccadilly. Farther east is Burlington House, to the west Devonshire House, on the site of the former Berkeley House, destroyed by fire.

In the early years of this past century there were only two houses of importance in the eastern stretch of Piccadilly – Clarges House and Townshend House, the latter becoming Sunderland House and then York House when Lord Sunderland exchanged houses with the King's second son, Frederick, Duke of York; now there are plans to alter and enlarge York House – which the Duke has left – and to let it out as bachelors' chambers, the building to be called 'The Albany' (the Prince is Duke of Albany as well as of York).

On the south side of Piccadilly, where the Green Park ends, is Arlington Street, and close by is the White Horse Cellar, head-quarters of the coaches driving westwards. St James's Street,

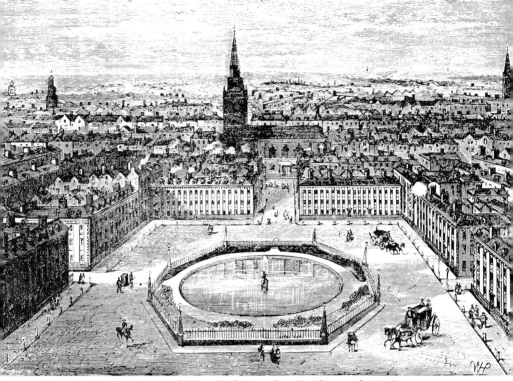

St James's Square showing the new fountain

running down to St James's Palace, is opposite Albemarle Street, the site of the old Clarendon House, and farther east is the church of St James, which Wren said he liked the best of all his churches, having designed it to be 'so capacious as with pews and galleries to hold two thousand persons, and all to hear the service and see the preacher'.

Shops are beginning to appear in this part of Piccadilly, one of the earliest being Fortnum & Mason's – Mr Fortnum, a footman in the service of Queen Anne, set up his shop with Mr Mason in 1707. Close by is Hatchard's, the book shop. John Hatchard spent his boyhood at the Greycoat School and in 1784 was apprenticed to Mr Ginger, the bookseller to Westminster School. He did well and only three years ago opened his own shop here in Piccadilly. Already it has become a meeting-place for men of letters, particularly those who are members of the Tory party.

There has been a good deal of building along Piccadilly during the last few years, although no houses on the scale of the earlier mansions. The house on the corner of Stratton Street was built in the 1760s for Lord Eglinton, and five years ago it was bought for Thomas Coutts, the banker, who, after the death of his first wife, married the Drury Lane actress Harriet Mellon. 80 Piccadilly, next to the Coutts' house, was built by Sir Richard Lyttelton in 1764. 81, on the east corner of Bolton Street, was built in the 1750s but is now standing empty. There are several more houses along this stretch of Piccadilly, all occupied by distinguished people. Sir Thomas Lawrence, recently appointed painter to the King, lived at 102 until two years ago, and the diplomat Sir William Hamilton has just taken the lease of a house nearby, with his wife Emma. William Douglas, fourth Duke of Queensbury, a sportsman known to all the world as 'Old Q', built 138 for himself, in 1768, and has lived here ever since.

There has always been a good deal of speculation about the origin of the name Piccadilly. Early in the seventeenth century, Robert Baker, a tailor from the Strand, bought a small plot of land in the tangle of streets and alleys lying between Piccadilly and the Haymarket. Here he built his house which was called Piccadilly Hall – 'piccadills' were ruffs which had become high fashion for men, and Taylor must have specialized in them and sold dozens at his Strand shop. There was also a kind of cake called a piccadilla very popular about that time, which could well have been named after the ruff.

Passing due east from Piccadilly, the best way to reach Leicester Fields – now known as Leicester Square – is to go down Whitcomb Street and reach the south side of the square by way of Spur Street. Most of the north side of the square is occupied by Leicester House, which George III's father, Frederick, Prince of Wales, built soon after the birth of the future King. To reach Cockspur Street and the Strand, go down the Haymarket.

The Strand, with Hungerford market on your right, is very narrow until about Burlington Street and then widens somewhat, and behind it to the north is Inigo Jones's development of Covent Garden, with its piazza and theatres, approached from the Strand by Half Moon Street, leading to Bedford Street, Catherine Street and Drury Lane. On the river side of the Strand are Somerset House and the ruins of the Savoy Palace.

The people of wealth and fashion who used to inhabit Covent Garden when it was first built are moving westwards into Mayfair these days, leaving the square and its surrounding streets to theatre people, dramatists and writers.

In the Strand, all the mansions of medieval days have disappeared or – like the Savoy Palace – lie in ruins; only the Chapel, now 300 years old, is still standing. Old Somerset House was demolished early in this past century; Sir William Chambers began work on the present Somerset House about twenty-five years ago, but it has not been used as a residence. Part has been taken over for government offices, and in the north front the annual exhibition of the Royal Academy has been held for the last twenty years. However, in the extreme western part of the Strand, the seventeenth-century Northumberland House, home of the Percys of Northumberland for 200 years, still stands – a vast, gloomy-looking place but splendid inside, with a magnificent ballroom, more than a hundred feet long, an outstandingly beautiful staircase, some 150 rooms and extensive riverside gardens.

The Wren Church of St Clement Danes marks the point where the Strand meets Fleet Street. Continuing eastwards, we approach Ludgate Hill, at whose foot Farringdon Street runs north to Holborn. It was built in 1737 over the Fleet ditch, which still flows beneath it into the Thames.

Before beginning the climb up Ludgate Hill, pause to glance at the Fleet prison, at the bottom, on your left, which has been here for more than 600 years, although it was rebuilt after the Great Fire of 1666 and rebuilt again only twenty years ago, after it had been damaged by fire during the Gordon Riots.

Ludgate Hill is lined with splendid mercers' and drapers' shops, and de Saussure made special mention of them after his visit to London, saying that he thought Ludgate Hill, the Strand, Fleet Street, Cheapside and Cornhill the finest streets in all Europe.

On the left side of Ludgate Hill is the Belle Sauvage inn. This was once the Bell Inn, which early in the seventeenth century was run by the Savage family, but its name has a more romantic origin . . .

John Rolfe, a member of the Virginia Company working in the colony of Virginia, married the Indian Princess Pocahontas. In 1616 he brought her back to London, where she met King James I, Queen Anne and Sir Walter Raleigh and was an object of great wonder and curiosity to the citizens of London. John Rolfe took his wife to stay at the Savages' inn, the Bell, but Pocahontas did not long survive the fog and damp of the city, and in 1617 she died. After that time, the Bell became known as the 'Belle Sauvage' – 'the Beautiful Savage', and the Savages hung up a portrait of Pocahontas as their inn sign.

The magnificent St Paul's Cathedral stands at the top of the hill, serenely dominating all the surrounding streets and buildings.

Skirting the north side of St Paul's and passing along Cheapside and Poultry, we arrive at the hub of the City – the spot where Threadneedle Street, Cornhill, Lombard Street and Poultry meet. Here, on the corner of Prince's Street and Threadneedle Street, is

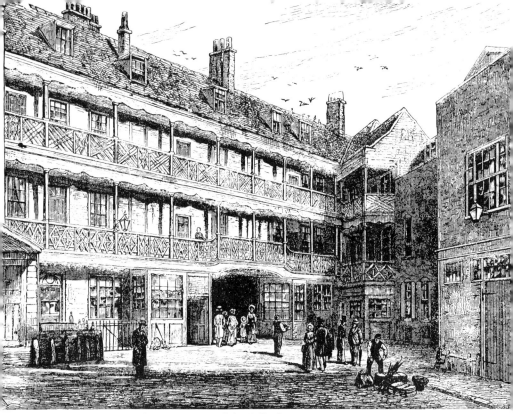

The inner court of the Belle Sauvage

the Bank of England, built in 1734, when it moved from its first home in the Grocers' Hall.

The Bank is built on the site of the house and garden of Sir John Houblon, one of the Bank's first directors. The house could not be seen from the street, being approached through an archway into a courtyard, and built closely round it were the church of St Christopher le Stocks, with its burial ground, three taverns and some fifteen or twenty small houses. These were all pulled down, but the burial ground was preserved, to become the Bank's central garden, and the story goes that, soon after its establishment, permission was granted for one of the clerks, who was seven feet six inches tall, to be buried there in order to save his body from the grave-robbers who were so prevalent in those times – indeed, they still are, snatching newly buried corpses to sell to anatomists for dissection and research into their developing science.

The original Bank building was designed by George Sampson, and the east and west wings were added a few years later by Sir Robert Taylor, but Sir John Soane, who was appointed architect twelve years ago, was mainly responsible for the present magnificent building of pillared courtyards, beautiful halls and court

39

rooms. The work on the north façade was begun only five years ago and is not yet completed.

During the Gordon Riots, twenty years ago, the mob rampaged through the City, burning and looting on the way, and then they advanced on the Bank, hoping to reach the vaults where the bullion was stored, but horse and foot guards arrived just in time to drive them back, and to this day a detachment of guards rides over every evening, at six o'clock.

On the corner of Threadneedle Street and Cornhill is the Royal Exchange. The Tudor Exchange was lost in the Great Fire, and this second Exchange, built on the same site, by Edward Jerman, is considerably larger. It is a quadrangle with a wide, open court, 144 feet by 147 feet, surrounded by a colonnade – there are also colonnades on the north and south sides of the building which, when it was first opened, contained 160 shops. The entrance portico faces Cornhill, and from it rises a three-storey tower, with a four-dialled clock in the second storey, which rings out a tune four times a day, the tune being different for every day of the week. Surmounting the tower is a grasshopper, the family crest of Sir Thomas Gresham, the Exchange's founder.

'There is no place in the town which I so much love to frequent as the Royal Exchange,' wrote Joseph Addison, the essayist, who died in 1719. 'It gives me a secret satisfaction, and in some measure gratifies my vanity, as I am an Englishman, to see so rich an assembly of countrymen and foreigners consulting together upon the private business of mankind and making this metropolis a kind of emporium for the whole earth. . . . I have often been pleased to hear the disputes adjusted between an inhabitant of Japan and an alderman of London; or to see a subject of the great Mogul entering into a league with one of the Tsars of Muscovy. . . .'

Addison's contemporary, Sir Richard Steele, writing in *The Tatler*, described his adventures in the shops at the Change: 'It was not the least of my satisfaction in my survey to go upstairs and pass the shops of agreeable females,' he wrote. 'To observe so many pretty hands busy in the folding of ribbons and the utmost eagerness of agreeable faces in the sale of patches, pins and wires, on each side of the counters, was an amusement in which I could longer have indulged myself, had not the dear creatures called to me, to ask what I wanted.'

But the shops did not pay and were gradually forsaken. Steele records that, 'On evening Change the mumpers [beggars], the halt, the blind, and the lame; your vendors of trash, apples, plums; your ragamuffins, rake-shales [libertines] and wenches – have

40

Sir Richard Steele's old house at Haverstock Hill

jostled the greater number of honourable merchants, substantial tradesmen and knowing masters of ships, out of that place. So that what with the din of quarrelling, oaths, and cries of beggars, men of the greatest consequence in our City absent themselves from the Royal Exchange.'

The inside shops of the Exchange have now been removed and in their place have been established the Royal Exchange Assurance Offices, Lloyd's Coffee-House, the Mercantile Seaman's Offices, the Gresham Lecture Room and the Lord Mayor's Court Office, while the outside shops have become lottery offices, newspaper offices, watchmakers and notaries. Some of the vaults are let to bankers and the rest to the East India Company, for the storage of their pepper imports.

Opposite the Bank of England is the Lord Mayor's residence, the Mansion House, which was completed in 1755. (Until that time, the Lord Mayor had resided in his own house in the City.) It is a massive building, with a central courtyard, a banqueting hall ('the Egyptian Room', large enough for 400 guests), smaller dining-rooms, a great drawing-room, a ballroom, and the room containing the State bed (which alone cost 3,000 guineas). The first Lord Mayor to live in the Mansion House, Sir Crisp Gascoigne, cele-brated moving in with an enormous feast: 'The first course at dinner consisted of six hundred covered dishes from the kitchen alone, exclusive of other eatables, and in the whole the number of dishes sent up is said to have exceeded upwards of 1,000.' The next Lord Mayor died of 'gout in the stomach' only three weeks after taking office.

Soon after occupation, the Mansion House was found to be not only uncomfortable as a residence but extremely damp – it is built on piles, on soft ground over subterranean springs. One after another, Lord Mayors have complained about it, and seven years ago the Common Council seriously considered building a new house on another site. The son of the original architect, George Dance the Younger, who had succeeded his late father as City Surveyor, suggested that the central courtyard be covered, '. . . thus furnishing a noble and convenient access to the Egyptian Hall as well as rendering the House free from the dampness which now exists'. This has been done and has proved effective, but there are still complaints about the unsightly attic floor above the ballroom, which is generally referred to as the 'Noah's Ark' or 'the Mayor's Nest'. It spoils the balance of the building and one day it will probably be removed.

The Mansion House is the only palatial residence left in the City of London. The mansions of the gentry who once lived here have all disappeared now, the sites used for more commercial building. Many former residents have taken houses in the west end of London or the squares of Mayfair, for the winter 'Season'. However, the City merchants live in large and comfortable houses, which are also their offices, the apprentices working on the ground floor and the merchant and his family living in the floors above.

Running northwards from the eastern end of Cheapside is King Street, which was built after the Great Fire of 1666 and leads to Guildhall Yard and the Guildhall. The hall was badly damaged during the fire and lost its medieval open-timbered roof, but it was not totally destroyed and was restored, with an attic storey and flat, panelled roof. But parts of the old hall are nearly 400 years old now, and the restorations by George Dance eleven years ago are by no means satisfactory. The magnificent old crypt is quite neglected, being used at the present time merely as a storage place for the benches and trestles which are brought out for City banquets.

From the south side of the Royal Exchange, Cornhill runs eastwards, ending in Leadenhall Street. Lombard Street runs south-eastwards from the Exchange, to continue as Fenchurch Street, which swings north-eastwards, with Mark Lane turning off

Interior of the Egyptian Hall at the Mansion House

to the south, to meet Great Tower Street and the Tower of London, and Fenchurch Street continues north-eastwards to Whitechapel.

The Stock Exchange is establ hed at Jonathan's Coffee-House in Change Alley, off Cornhill.

East of Aldgate and Whitechapel there is little building, but to the north-west are Spitalfields and its market. Farther east and in the north-east, in Bethnal Green, Mile End and Stepney, which many remember as open countryside, houses and streets are just beginning to appear.

North of Gresham Street and the Guildhall, facing the site of the old London Wall, is the Bethlem (Bedlam) Hospital for the insane, and behind it are Moorfields, Middle Moorfields and Upper Moorfields. To the east of Upper Moorfields is the Artillery Ground, and beyond it, to the north, Tindal's burying ground, reaching to the sparsely populated Old Street and Hoxton and the fields of Middlesex. To the west is Bloomsbury, which was built about the same time as Mayfair – its charming squares are a fashionable place of residence, although generally speaking the houses are not so grand as the Mayfair mansions. North of Blooms-bury, Lamb's Conduit Fields stretch northwards towards the Marylebone Gardens again.

Until fifty years ago, the City had only one bridge – London Bridge. It had been restored to great splendour in Tudor times, and at the Southwark end a new gate was built and the tower, three storeys high, with the covered way below; over the seventh and eighth arches on the north side of the drawbridge was built Nonesuch House. But it sorely needed more repair.

A project for a second bridge between Westminster and Lambeth had been proposed two years before the Great Fire, but the City opposed the idea, anxious that the traffic and trade which passed through London should remain concentrated on London Bridge. It was not until 1750 that, after eleven years in the building, West-minster Bridge was opened, running from New Palace Yard to the Surrey side of the river. The City protested, as did some of the taverners of Southwark and the Thames watermen, but they were overruled by the Archbishop of Canterbury, who had grown tired of the old ferry service between Lambeth Palace and Westminster. Financed by Parliamentary grants and public lotteries, the new bridge is very elegant, designed by the Swiss architect Charles Labelye, but already it is suggested that some of the piers are not safe.

Blackfriars Bridge, built from the design of a young Scotsman,

The Mansion House, from an old print prepared for Stow's Survey of London

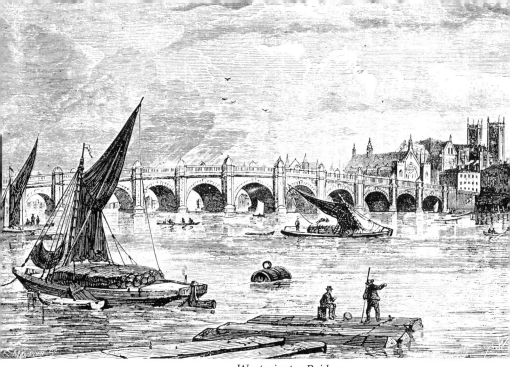
Westminster Bridge

Robert Mylne, was begun in 1760 and opened in November 1769 –
it is considered the most beautiful in the whole country.

At the same time, the Fleet Ditch was filled in and the crumbling
old Roman walls of the City were pulled down and the gates
removed. But old London Bridge still stands. The buildings have
been cleared away, for the houses had become dangerously dilapidated and the shops no longer fashionable, the mercers and
drapers having departed, leaving only little haberdashery shops to
which economical ladies still drive from the west end of the town to
make cheap purchases. Forty years ago, Sir Robert Taylor and
George Dance the elder set about repairing the bridge, cutting it in
two and building a new, wide central arch, but the join soon
became so insecure that people hesitated to venture over it. Stones
from the old City gates were used to strengthen the foundations of
the new arch, but they soon became loose again, because of the
scouring of the current. The repairs of the bridge are costing £2,500
a year now, and a new bridge is urgently needed, but nothing has
yet been done about it – and the children still sing, with good
reason, 'London Bridge is falling down.'

George Griffin Stonestreet has this year published his criticisms
of London as it is today. He complains of the carelessness which
causes so many fires. The pavement is broken on Fish Street Hill
and should be repaired, either at night time, by torchlights, or on

46

Sundays, when it is not much in use. St Saviour's Church in Southwark has fallen into ruins and has just been left as a heap of rubble. The whole area from Southwark High Street in the east to Blackfriars Bridge in the west, from the banks of the river all the way back to St George's Fields, is potentially good building land but today is nothing but a chaos of dirty, crooked streets, narrow lanes, alleys and laystalls, which it is impossible to explore without regret and astonishment. The siting of Union Street, Southwark, built only twenty years ago, he considers to be unintelligent, being nothing more than a line from Nowhere to Nowhere. The City Monument, he says, was placed inconveniently at the side and foot of a hill. Of the Bethlem Hospital, he asks: 'How long is that spectacle of misery to remain on such a valuable piece of building land? Why not remove it to the other great lunatic hospital in Old Street?'

Stonestreet also complains that the streets are very untidy around Temple Bar and that Spitalfields is sadly decaying since the weavers have been put out of business by the invention of the power loom and departed. He also recommends the removal of the Fleet market, but finally and most insistently he says: 'We must have a new bridge either of stone or iron – to replace London Bridge *immediately*.'

London Bridge in 1796

3. Transport

Arthur Young, a writer on agriculture and rural life, deplores the beginning of an exodus from the countryside to London, attributing it to the improved roads. In his published *Farmer's Letters*, he writes:

> To find fault with good roads would have the appearance of paradox and absurdity; but it is nevertheless a fact that giving the power of expeditious travelling depopulates the Kingdom. Young men and women in the country villages fix their eyes on London as the last stage of their hope. They enter into service in the country for little else but to raise money enough to go to London, which was no such easy matter when a stage-coach was four or five days in creeping an hundred miles. The fare and the expenses ran high. *But now*! a country fellow, one hundred miles from London, jumps on a coach box in the morning, and for eight or ten shillings gets to town by night, which makes a material difference; besides rendering the going up and down so easy, the numbers *who have seen London* are increased tenfold, and of course ten times the boasts are sounded in the ears of country fools to induce them to quit their healthy clean fields for a region of dirt, stink and noise.

The journey between London and Bath can now be accomplished in seventeen hours, at an average speed of six miles an hour, and with breakfast, dinner and tea on the way will cost £4.9s.6d. Five years ago a traveller leaving London at four o'clock in the morning arrived at Bath at eleven o'clock the same evening – nineteen hours, while thirty-five years ago the same journey took twenty-nine hours.

Although there are commercial coach routes between provincial cities, London sits at the centre of a web of national transport. Daily dozens of coaches depart for all parts of the country, both stage-coaches and mail-coaches. The latter are the faster mode of public transport, and those with urgent business obviously choose to travel by mail-coach, as do those carrying valuables, for the Royal Mail is well guarded by armed men, but many people still prefer the more leisurely stage-coach – partly for fear of accidents at high speed, partly in order to enjoy the over-night stops at wayside inns which stage-coach travel affords.

It was, in fact, the staging system which first promoted speedy travel, when it became the custom to change horses *en route*, rather than use the same, tired horses for the whole journey. Certain inn-keepers are contracted to provide this change of horse – not a lucrative business in itself, but they make profit from travellers who dine or stay overnight at their houses.

Another factor in faster travel is the recent improvement in road surfaces – though there is still a long way to go before Britain has a satisfactory network of first-class roads. Some thirty years ago Arthur Young, already quoted, complained vigorously of the state of the road between Preston and Wigan over which he travelled: 'I know not in the whole range of the language, terms sufficiently expressive to describe this infernal road . . . let me most seriously caution all travellers who may accidentally purpose to travel this terrible country to avoid as they would the devil; for a thousand to one but they break their neck or their limbs by overthrow or breaking down. They will meet with ruts, which I actually measured four feet deep. . . . I passed three carts broken down in these eighteen miles of execrable memory.'

Since that time the increase in the number of Turnpike Trusts has brought about an improvement – and has taken the burden of payment for road repairs off local people, who formerly complained vociferously against having to pay for the upkeep of roads used by strangers on their travels. Turnpike Trusts are small companies empowered by Parliament to erect gates and toll bars on the roads, at which they exact a fee from riders and coach-travellers, using a stipulated percentage of the money received to pay for the upkeep of roads. It has been estimated that today there are no fewer than 8,000 tollgates on the roads.

Inevitably, travellers complain of delays at tollgates and of the charges they have to meet, and there is widespread demand for the Government to take upon itself the care of the high-ways. Two Scotsmen, Thomas Telford and John McAdam, have experimented with new methods of road construction, using a rubble base infilled with stone chips, and then surfaced, and their innovation may well become the basis for a new national road network in the nineteenth century.

A third factor in improved means of travel is the experimentation of coachmakers. Apart from the heavy coaches used to transport long-distance travellers on commercial routes, there are now many varieties of lighter coaches more suited to town use.

The Fountain Inn in the Minories, near Tower Hill

The post-chaise is popular and comfortable for long journeys, the body hanging by leather braces to upright springs. The back wheels are considerably larger than the front wheels, and luggage is stacked both in front and behind. But the smart thing today is the phaeton for two, drawn by two horses. The perch phaeton, with the body immediately over the front wheels, is a sporting design but rather dangerous. The gig, drawn by one horse, has only two wheels, the open body being suspended by leather braces from curved springs. A two-horse gig is known as a curricle, and if it has a hood it is a cabriolet. Another form, with a different arrangement of springs, is known as a whisky.

London thoroughfares are frequently choked with these small carriages, vying for room with the wagons of artisans and traders and with the stage- and mail-coaches departing from the city. Thus wherever it is practicable the Thames is still used for the movement of heavy goods, and an Act of Parliament was passed five years ago for the provision of a canal, starting at Paddington, which will link up with the Grand Junction Canal which serves the industrial Midlands.

Nevertheless, even those who complain of London's congested and often dangerous streets enjoy the sight of the mail-coach departures every evening, and, in summer, crowds gather to watch them.

'The finest sight in the metropolis is the setting off of the mail coaches from Piccadilly,' wrote the young William Hazlitt. 'The horses paw the ground and are impatient to be gone, as if conscious of the precious burden they convey. The mail carts drive up and the transfer of packages is made, and at a given signal off they start. . . . Some persons think that the noblest object in Nature is the ship launched on the bosom of the ocean; but give me, for my private satisfaction, the mail coaches that pour down Piccadilly of an evening, tear up the pavement and devour the way before them to *The Land's End*.'

From the General Post Office in Lombard Street all the mail-coaches (except those bound for the west) depart every evening at eight o'clock, having first loaded up their passengers and luggage from the inns. To avoid congestion, passengers for the West Country assemble at booking offices and inns in Oxford Street and Piccadilly or are taken there in coaches from their City inns, while the guards collect their mail boxes from the Post Office and drive down to the West End departure points to join the mail-coaches. There is a line of inns from the City to the West End, catering for these west-bound coaches and their passengers, including the Green Man and Still and the Gloucester Coffee-House in Oxford Street, for those using the Uxbridge road, the White Bear, the Spread Eagle, the Bull and Mouth and the Golden Cross in Piccadilly for the Hounslow route. Hatchett's is another popular coaching inn for travellers to the West Country, as is the White Horse Cellar, on the corner of Arlington Street, which is considered one of the finest inns in London.

Today the principal coaching inns in London are the Bull and Mouth, St Martin's-le-Grand, the Belle Sauvage on Ludgate Hill, the Swan With Two Necks, Lad Lane, the Spread Eagle in Gracechurch Street, the White Horse in Fetter Lane, the Blossom Inn, Lawrence Lane, Cheapside, the Bolt-in-Tun, Fleet Street, the Cross Keys, Wood Street, Cheapside, the Golden Cross, Charing Cross, the George and Blue Boar in Holborn, the Bell and Crown, Holborn, the Bull Inn, Aldgate, the Three Nuns, Aldgate, and the Saracen's Head and King's Arms, both on Snow Hill. All these inns have stabling for bringing in horses late at night and taking them out early in the morning, as well as stables for the night coach and mail-horses which stay in London all day.

The Belle Sauvage (already mentioned on p. 38) has become a magnificent inn, its galleried courtyard busy with the fast day and night coaches running to Bath, Cheltenham, Brighton, Cambridge and Manchester, and carrying the Newmarket-Norwich mail. It stables 400 horses and is renowned for its comfort and good food, although a few years ago, when Parson Woodforde stayed there, he had certain reservations about the comfort: 'They were very civil people and a very good House it is,' he recorded, but he added: 'I

Mail coach at the White Bear Inn, Piccadilly

The Cambridge coach setting off from La Belle Sauvage on Ludgate Hill

was bit terribly by the buggs last night, but did not wake me.' Four years later he had the same trouble: 'I was bit so terribly with buggs again this night that I got up at four o'clock this morning and took a long walk by myself about the City till breakfast time.' The following night, he said, 'I did not pull off my cloathes . . . but sat up in a Great Chair all night with my Feet on the bed and slept very well considering and not pestered with buggs.'

Since London has become such a wide-spread city, many citizens and visitors do not care to walk the long distances from, say, Mayfair to the Tower, or even from the shops of the West End to the inn at which they lodge in the East End, so that the drivers of hackneyed – that is, hired – coaches ply a lucrative trade. The first hackney coach rank appeared in London in 1634, forming at the maypole in the Strand. Today's neat, comfortable vehicles are a vast improvement on the 'hell-carts' of the early years, which had no springs and no windows, the only protection from the weather being flapping leather curtains. They caused terrible traffic jams in the narrow streets, and when two met head-on there was no room to give way. Wheels came off and coaches overturned. Drivers haggled over fares and drove too fast. There was an attempt to suppress them, but the coachmen had no intention of going out of business, and within a few weeks, after much argument and protest, fifty hackney coachmen were licensed again, being allowed twelve horses each.

Restoration London saw a rival to the hackney carriage in the sedan chair – a single seat enclosed in a 'box', supported by poles carried by two men. While some people welcomed the sedan as a possible solution to the traffic problem which London suffered even then, others professed 'a loathing that men should be brought to as servile a condition as horses'. Nevertheless, as both private and public transport, the sedan flourished in the first half of the past century, and though they are now going out of fashion, there is still a stand for about half a dozen in St James's Street.

4. Food and Drink

The basic diet of British peasants is bread and cheese, with meat when times are good, fish when they can catch it, and game when it comes their way – probably by poaching, and with them they take fruit and vegetables if they have the land on which to grow them. Except for the really unfortunate and destitute, food is in abundance and variety.

With the recent introduction of winter feeding for cattle, meat is plentiful, and enormous quantities are eaten by the majority of people, particularly beef, but also veal, mutton and lamb. Venison is for the landed gentry, who often distribute gifts of it to their neighbours and friends. Poultry is cheap and plentiful, and so is fish. The Londoner's salmon is caught at the fishery at Putney, and London fishermen make a good living from the Thames. Large country households have well-stocked fishponds for the coarser fish, such as carp, perch, tench and eels, and as transport improves, supplies from the coast reach ever farther inland by way of Billingsgate market. Dairy products are plentiful, and it is usual for quite small households to keep a cow and make their own butter and cheese.

Sugar, sometimes in large loaves weighing as much as twenty-two pounds, dried fruit and spices, including pepper, nutmeg and cinnamon, are imported regularly and are easily available in grocers' shops. Nearly all gardens have a vegetable patch as well as fruit trees and sometimes nut trees, so for many their diet includes apples, nectarines, peaches, strawberries, apricots, pears, filberts and walnuts. Imported lemons and oranges are quite cheap, but the more exotic fruits, particularly pineapples, are very expensive. In the kitchen gardens are potatoes, green vegetables, carrots, onions, turnips, cucumbers and salads.

The diet of everyone, from the moderately prosperous to the wealthy, also includes pies of all kinds, with a variety of sweets and puddings.

Some people still refrain from eating meat during Lent, eating instead red herrings and salt fish, with perhaps leeks, parsnips and peas, but roast lamb is nearly always served at Easter time, with veal, a gammon bacon and a tansy pudding on Easter day, while gooseberry pie appears at Whitsuntide, and turkey, mince pies and plum porridge at Christmas.

Cooking is done on an open fire. In most kitchens a joint is trussed onto a revolving spit which is suspended over the fire by hooks attached to firedogs (andirons). The fat is caught in a dripping pan, and the spit is turned either by hand or by a simple mechanical device.

Pots and kettles hang from large iron hooks above the fireplace, and frying pans and saucepans are set over the fire on trivets. Bread is baked in an oven built into the brickwork of the chimney. This is first heated with a bundle of hot faggots, and when they are removed and the bread is put in, the oven is closed with an iron door. Bacon is smoked and cured in a smoke chamber in the flue of the fire and built at the side of the chimney.

In country districts, where difficulties of transport make coal expensive and wood is used for fuel, the fire seldom goes out, the ashes remaining in the hearth and stirred into life again each morning. In London, however, coal has been used as domestic fuel for many years. About twenty years ago, the first kitchen range was designed, with an oven built on the side of an open fire. This meant that one side of the food cooked more than the other, so shelves were devised, which twisted on a pivot. The very latest idea is to fit a boiler for hot water on the other side of the range, but it has to be filled by hand; some ranges have recently been provided with a cover to the fire, which serves as a hot plate and is invaluable for boiling and stewing.

Sophie v. la Roche often mentions British food in letters home to her daughters. At the British hotel at Helvoetsluys, while awaiting the crossing to Harwich, their lunch, she said, consisted of 'soup, some good-sized fish, large English roasts, vegetables boiled in salted water, with melted butter; pastries, fruit and a large cheese, served in a beautifully carved mahogany cart and rolled on four brass castors from one guest to another'.

At Ingatestone, on the way from Harwich to London, they enjoyed their first English supper 'immensely'. They were given 'slices of beef and veal, cut very thin and beaten tender, about the size of a hand, sprinkled with bread crumbs and grilled, and nicely served on a silver dish, fine big potatoes with salt butter to follow, delicious beer and a good Bordeaux wine'. She also volunteers the information that, 'A pound of beef costs eight-pence here. Likewise a pound of butter; twenty-four eggs are

Kitchen of St James's Palace

a shilling, a capon three shillings and a cow seven guineas.'

Arrived in London and walking one day from the Strand to Leicester Fields, she records that, 'A pastry cook's attracted our attention for some time, as it is surrounded, like a large spacious room, by glass cases, in which all kinds of preserved fruits and jellies are exhibited in handsome glass jars; in the middle of the shop, however, there stood a big table with a white cover containing a pyramid of small pastries and tartlets and some larger pastries and sweetmeats; wine glasses of all sizes, with lids to them, and full of liqueurs of every conceivable brand, colour and taste, were attractively set out in between, as might be expected, at a large and very elegant table. What we women liked best of all, though, was a large but delightful covering made of gauze, which hid nothing from view and at the same time kept the flies off.'

57

She lunched with the Count Cagliostro at his home in Knightsbridge, where, 'The menu was half Italian and half English. In place of soup, with which we were served, Cagliostro took macaroni. Then stewed lamb, fresh young codling, steamed cabbage, pork, a large fish, mussels, roast veal, a huge loin chop and a heap of cress, potatoes in thick brown sauce, a salad and pastries. The table was covered with a fine big damask cloth, on which we all wiped our mouths in old English style, as there were no serviettes. The dishes were silver, the plates china, and the glasses of English crystal. The costliest wines were at our command.'

It is the custom in larger households for the soup and fish to be served at the same time as the roasts. Everything is put on the table at the beginning of the meal. Guests help themselves to what they fancy, and the same plate does for everything. The servants eat what is left, for they are not catered for separately but eat the same food as the family. The wine is not put on the table during the meal, but you ask for what you would like from the display of bottles on the sideboard. That is why Sophie says that, 'The costliest wines were at our command.' Within the last few years hosts have begun to place the wine on the table at the beginning of the meal, but, as one writer has recently remarked, 'The new custom is far from being general.'

When Sophie lunched with Mr Heinselmann, a relation of her mother's, they had a simpler 'old English menu', consisting of '. . . a large fish, boiled mutton, pudding, boiled cabbage with butter and a roast. Punch was made at the table.'

There are many varieties of punch, all of them potent. The basic recipe for common punch, made in quantity, is thirty-six peeled lemons, two pounds of loaf sugar, three quarts of sherbert, a pint of brandy and a pint of rum; in another variety, gin is used instead of brandy and rum. Rumfustian is made from twelve whisked eggs, to which are added a quart of strong beer, a pint of gin, a bottle of sherry, nutmeg, sugar and the rind of a lemon.

Sophie visited Covent Garden, where the fruit and vegetable market is spreading so quickly these days that it has almost filled the three acres of Inigo Jones' beautiful square. There are shops and booths along the south and east side, while in the middle and along the north side is an untidy collection of booths and tumbledown sheds, in many of which the market people are now living. So, amongst the fruit and vegetables, some butchers' and bakers' shops have opened, to supply their needs.

Sophie had never eaten oysters and decided to try them one day, after a visit to the Tower of London, when they came to a fish

Early morning in Covent Garden

market near the Customs House, where a load of oysters had just arrived:

> . . . some people were eagerly buying and carrying them off, while others had them opened and were eating them, for innumerable bread and lemon vendors were present, offering their services. For a time we watched with interest, finally we were seized by the desire to sample really fresh oysters. We entered an inn, where the lower floor was separated off into a number of small rooms holding six or eight persons. The cubicles were neat, the tables laid with white cloths, and there were delightful wicker chairs to sit in. A fisher-woman with a basket of oysters, a youngster with lemons and a small basket containing bread, plates and knives followed immediately after us. An excited enthusiasm whispered in my ear: 'These are English oysters and you are in London', and any previous aversion to oyster-eating I may have entertained vanished, and I liked them very much.

When she was invited to the home of the Count and Countess of Reventlow at Richmond, a family of four joined them, and Sophie remarked that, 'A complete English repast suggested the reason why such large dishes are to be seen in silver, pewter, china and crockery shops; to wit, because a quarter of a calf, half a lamb and monstrous pieces of meat are dished up, and everyone receives almost an entire fish.'

It has been estimated that today London consumes each year 2,957,000 bushels of wheaten flour, 100,000 oxen, 700,000 sheep and lambs, 195,000 calves, 238,000 pigs, 115,000 bushels of oysters, 14,000,000 mackerel, 16,000,000 pounds of butter and 21,000 pounds of cheese – apart from game and poultry.

Food is flavoured with fruit and herbs, gooseberries are served with mackerel, fennel with crab, lobster and salmon, quince with apple pie, sweet rosemary with boar's head, not forgetting an orange or pippin to stick in his mouth, currants with veal, and honey with beef.

For those who take a meal at a cookshop or tavern, 1½d will buy enough bread to last a man a whole day. A few years ago, a needy young man could take his food with a mixed company of footmen and chairmen for 3½d, and if he were very short of cash he could even pick up a sausage at a farthing 'fry', while at an 'ordinary' he could have a very good meal for anything from 6d to a shilling.

Dr Johnson, when he first came to London in 1737, used to dine for 8d at the Pineapple in New Street, Covent Garden, giving 6d for a cut of meat, 1d for bread and 1d for the waiter. But when he was established and working on his dictionary, at his house in Gough Square, he usually took dinner at the Cheshire Cheese, just off Fleet Street, in Wine Office Court. Oliver Goldsmith, living at 6 Wine Office Court and earning a precarious living writing for the booksellers, joined him when he could afford to, and they always sat in the same corner by the window. The Cheshire Cheese is still renowned for its good food, the favourite dish being their beef-steak pudding, which is served on Saturdays. It is said to contain, piled into the suet crust in a huge basin, beefsteaks, kidneys, oysters, larks, mushrooms, and wondrous spices and herbs, and there is a story going the rounds that on a windy day, the smell of it has been known to reach as far as the Stock Exchange.

The 'lunch' to which Sophie refers was the main meal of the day, which we call dinner. Meal times vary but, generally speaking, breakfast is a light meal of tea and bread and butter. Labourers on rising have a mug of beer or tea and some bread. A few years ago, when times were better for them than they are today, they might have had meat or cheese as well. They take similar food with them for their midday meal and have their main meal of the day in the early evening, when work is finished. For the rest of the population, breakfast is equally light, and the main meal – dinner – about three o'clock, followed by tea-drinking in the late afternoon and sometimes, though by no means always, supper about nine o'clock.

As the time of dinner grows later, people have taken to a mid-morning snack. In her diary, Sophie wrote: 'Since lunch in England is at four o'clock, supper generally falls out; at seven one partakes of tea and bread and butter; and the tea visits often last till eleven o'clock, when one goes home to an easy sleep undisturbed by indigestion.' Some people are now having dinner even later in the evening, however, and the mid-morning snack has become luncheon.

The national drink is beer, and the breweries of London produce more than 35 million gallons each year, but for centuries London has also been importing wine from the Continent. Today French, Spanish and Portuguese wines are drunk, as well as quantities of home-brewed ale, beer, porter, mead, cider and wine. Rum comes from the West Indies. French brandy is expensive, for it carries a heavy import duty, but large quantities are smuggled into the country.

Gin was introduced by William III. It is distilled from corn and was soon being produced in such vast amounts that it was cheaper than beer. In fact, its production required such large quantities of corn that farmers and large landowners reaped handsome profits. The poor developed a craving for it and drank it in inordinate amounts. It gave them an intoxication more complete and more destructive than the simple beer on which they had been nurtured. It robbed a man of his skill and dexterity: his hands began to shake; it destroyed his will and his natural affections; he pawned his tools, neglected his work, deserted his children. Women were trapped by it and also became addicts, selling the furniture and sending their children into the streets to live as best they could, or starve. There were gin shops everywhere – some of them just rough stalls put up at the corner of the street.

During the 1730s and 40s there were said to be between six and 7,000 gin shops in London. Drunken men and women lay about on the pavements, in the roads and in cellars, and they died in their hundreds. One dealer, near East Smithfield, had a large back room where, when his wretched customers grew helpless, they were laid out in heaps, men, women and children, until they recovered. As they woke, they thirsted for more gin, and if they had no money left, they went out to find some – 'and how they acquired more money the session papers too often acquainted us.'

When the middle and upper classes took to gin-drinking, the Government realized the urgent need for action. In 1751 an Act was passed decreeing a licence of £50 a year to sell gin and a duty of £1 a gallon, with a fine of £100 if the law were broken. This was stiff, for at the time British brandy was only 4 shillings a gallon, cognac 7s.9d, Jamaica rum 7s.6d, madeira from the West Indies 27 shillings and Valencia wine 3s.6d a gallon.

If the price of gin was far beyond the reach of the poor, so was that of the two popular non-alcoholic drinks – tea and coffee, but they managed to obtain supplies of smuggled tea and learnt to like it. It was not until sixteen years ago that William Pitt drastically reduced the import duty on tea, and smuggling was no longer worth the risks entailed, but until that time it was estimated that of the 12½ million pounds of tea consumed each year, duty had been paid on only 5 million. So now the poor drink tea, while gin is only for those who can afford it.

Both tea- and coffee-drinking have had an important influence on London's social life. Coffee became a popular drink in the East towards the end of the sixteenth century, and samples were soon arriving in Europe, where it was well liked. The first coffee-houses were opened in Constantinople and Venice, and in England the earliest recorded was at Oxford, in 1650.

London was sampling this new drink. When Mr Edwards, a merchant home from Smyrna served it to his friends, they liked it so much that he arranged for his Greek servant, Pasqua Rosée, to open a coffee-house for them in St Michael's Alley, off Cornhill. It quickly became very popular, and alehouse-keepers were so concerned that they petitioned the Lord Mayor, complaining that Pasqua Rosée was not a freeman and had no right to establish a business in the City, but after a lot of argument he was allowed to continue. Soon a rival was selling coffee close by, which he made in a simple booth, and here the customers were soon contributing 6d each, to enable him to build a proper coffee-house and engage an apprentice.

The fashion for coffee-drinking had arrived, despite the protests and vilifications of the brewers, who described the new drink as a syrup of soot and old shoes which made men unfruitful. The Government, too, was concerned for a time, for they feared that the coffee-houses would become breeding-grounds for sedition. Beer, they said, was preferable, because coffee was a stimulant which kept people awake and made them inclined to argument and rebellion, while beer kept them somnolent and loyal.

When, in 1656, James Farre, a barber, opened the Rainbow Coffee-House by Inner Temple Gate, in Fleet Street, the book-sellers prosecuted him '. . . for making and selling a drink called coffee, whereby in making the same, he annoyeth his neighbours, by evil smells, and for keeping of fire for the most part night and

A Mansion House Treat. A recent cartoon about smoking in London society

day, whereby his chimney and chamber hath been sett on fire, to the great danger and affrightment of his neighbours'. But they lost their case. Farre repaired his smoking chimney and continued to sell coffee, which his angry neighbours described as 'of a soote colour dryed in a furnace, that they drink as hotte as can be endured'.

Chocolate has long since been a fashionable drink, and as early as 1610 the Dutch East India Company imported a small consignment of China tea and found it approved as a pleasant drink and for its supposed medicinal properties. Then they introduced it to London, where it became just as popular for the few who could afford it – it cost anything up to £10 a pound. The English Company were soon bringing in their own supplies, and in 1657 Thomas Garraway, who ran a coffee-house in Exchange Alley, announced that he had acquired supplies of tea which he could sell from only 16 to 30 shillings a pound. When the Government imposed a tax of 5 shillings a pound on tea, smugglers began a trade in continental tea, which was selling for less than a shilling a pound. Businessmen would supply the capital for large purchases of tea (as well as brandy and tobacco), and the contraband was brought across the Channel and the North Sea to points off the south and east coasts. On moonless nights, fishing boats sailed out to meet the smugglers, and the tea was transferred and brought back to lonely beaches, where it was quickly unloaded and stored in barns, cellars and even churches, until the night riders were ready to set out on the long journey to London, their saddlebags heavy with their illicit cargo.

The penalty for smuggling was hanging but, of the hundreds of people who were involved, only a relatively small number were ever caught and brought to justice.

With the Restoration, the number of coffee-houses in London increased very quickly, particularly round the Royal Exchange and Covent Garden, where there were dozens – by Queen Anne's time there were said to be 500, of which 144 were within the City walls. And, as at Oxford, they soon became informal clubs, where men with similar interests met, to discuss their affairs and the news of the day. (Women were not allowed in the coffee houses, but took to tea-drinking in their own homes.) However, in some instances a fraternity of men with common interests formed their club and then chose the coffee-house which they would make their meeting place.

Today, the coffee-houses have become of true social importance to the country, for many more have developed into clubs. Tories meet at the Cocoa Tree, Whigs at the St James's Coffee-House – a Whig will no more go to the Cocoa Tree than a Tory will be seen at the coffee-house in St James's.

At Will's, in Covent Garden, the poet Dryden used to hold court in the late seventeenth century, and the company of his listeners and admirers became so distinguished that, although it had neither rules nor subscription, it is now regarded as one of London's first literary clubs. Several other coffee-houses in Covent Garden have become the meeting-places of intellectuals – as they drink, they gamble and talk endlessly, and often brilliantly. It was only for about ten years after Dryden's death, in 1700, that Will's maintained its old prestige. Then Button's, on the other side of Russell Street, had its day. It opened in 1712 and became the meeting-place of the writers Addison and Steele. Pope joined them here for a time but could not stand the pace. 'Addison usually studied all the morning,' recorded Pope, 'then joined the party at Button's, dined there, and stayed five or six hours; and sometimes far into the night. I was of the company for about a year, but found it too much for me; it hurt my health, and so I quitted it.'

Steele and Addison had already published *The Tatler*. Together they had produced the daily *Spectator*, and when they started work on the short-lived *Guardian*, they invited contributions to be sent to Button's. They placed at the entrance of the coffee-house a lion's head, with a large open mouth, into which aspiring authors were to place their contributions. These fell into the box held in the lion's paws, propped below its chin. 'Whatever the Lion swallows, I shall digest for the use of the public,' said Addison.

While Button's was at the height of its success, there was another coffee-house only a few doors away with an equally distinguished clientèle. This was Tom's, at 14 Russell Street, where there was playing at piquet, and the best of conversation till midnight. It was the resort of members of the Court and of the House of Lords. Tom's is still popular. Early in the 1760s a club was established there which included among its first members the actor David Garrick, the playwrights Foote, Murphy and Goldsmith, Dr Johnson ('the Great Lexicographer'), Admiral Lord Rodney, Lord Clive (famed for his work in India) and the Duke of Northumberland.

While many of the groups of politicians, artists, writers and actors who frequented the coffee-houses formed themselves into clubs, other coffee-houses degenerated into ordinary taverns. There were taverns which were as well run as the coffee-houses, but others were notorious for the evil doings of their frequenters. So it happened that in Covent Garden there were coffee-houses as disreputable as the worst of the taverns, and taverns where men of letters and distinction met regularly and innocuously.

Tom King's coffee-house, in front of St Paul's Church, Covent Garden, was one of the worst – little more than a brothel: Tom's widow, Moll, was arrested in 1739, charged with keeping a disorderly house and committed to the King's Bench prison; by the time she was released, the coffee-house had been pulled down.

The Finish, on the south side of the square, kept by Mrs Butler, was no better than Tom King's: here footpads and highwaymen used to mix with wealthy young bloods. Mother Douglas's, on the north side, was as bad, and the Rose in Russell Street had a name for being 'the resort of the worst characters of the town, both male and female, who made it the headquarters of midnight orgies and drunken broils, where murderous assaults were frequently occurring among the bullies of the time' – this is the place that the satirical artist Hogarth has depicted in his third scene of *The Rake's Progress*.

'Hell-fire' Stanhope's was equally notorious for gambling, wenching and cheap gin, prompting one enterprising rival

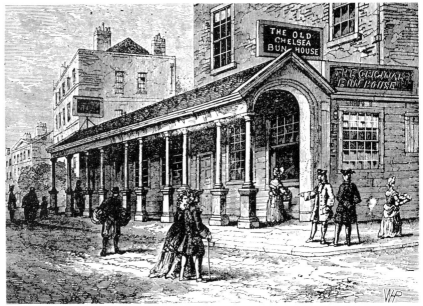

The Chelsea bun-house

tavernkeeper, according to Tobias Smollett, to put up a notice outside his establishment which read: 'Here you may get drunk for a penny, dead drunk for twopence, and get straw for nothing.'

It was at Rawthmell's coffee-house in Henrietta Street that the Society of Arts was founded, in 1754, and at number 23 was Offley's, famous for its Burton ale and the size and succulence of its mutton chops. Offley had once been employed at Bellamy's Chop and Coffee-House, adjoining the House of Commons, where members used to eat and drink and fill in time during dull debates, making it their club – today Offley's is Bellamy's greatest rival.

Within the City walls, many coffee-houses have become resorts for men of business, where deals are discussed and bargains sealed. For some years after the second Royal Exchange had opened, merchants met there and traded their wares by sample, the bulk of their goods being stored in the riverside warehouses, but as the coffee-houses grew in popularity, merchants deserted the Exchange, and individual coffee-houses have become associated with groups of common interests, often providing sale-rooms where their commodities can be auctioned.

The merchants in the West India trade (which includes sugar, rum and coffee) meet at the Jerusalem and Garraway's, both in Exchange Alley off Cornhill. The Virginia and Maryland coffee-house in Threadneedle Street is the meeting-place of merchants interested in the tobacco, sugar and cotton of the southern states of America. Close by is the Baltic, where men dealing in the Russian and Baltic trade in timber, oil, tallow, hemp and seeds do business. In 1744 the Virginia and Maryland joined forces with the Baltic and re-opened as the Virginia and Baltic. Tallow for candles is their most important commodity, and within the last few years they have been dealing in imported wheat, although with the fresh outbreak of the war with France, this side of the business is severely restricted these days.

West Indian merchandise is auctioned by sample at the Jerusalem and Garraway's, Garraway's having become the most important auction room for many foreign commodities. (It was there that the Hudson's Bay Company held their first auction of beaver skins.) Bidding is 'by candle': the auctioneer lights an inch of candle as a sign for bidding to begin, and it continues until the last flicker of flame, as the candle burns out. When the Company outgrew Garraway's, it moved to its present sale-room in Fenchurch Street.

Most of the East India Company's imports are sold at East India House in Fenchurch Street, which they built in 1726, but before that year they had premises on the same site. Pepper is particularly profitable, selling for 3d a pound in India and in London for 3 shillings a pound. Nowadays they also trade in snuff, saltpetre and small pieces of furniture, such as tables and screens, made of rare woods. Other items are cotton cloth, embroidered hangings, ivory, silk, brocades, arrack (an alcoholic drink from the East made from the areca nut or coco-palm), spices, cloves, nutmegs, mangoes, carpets and rugs; and the 'Indiamen' who go on to China and Japan for tea are now bringing back porcelain and beautifully painted Chinese wallpaper.

Marine assurers are the most important customers at Edward Lloyd's coffee-house in Lombard Street, and *Lloyd's List & Shipping Gazette* first appeared in 1734. Merchants with overseas interests and the ship-owners themselves all meet at Lloyd's, and assurers willing to insure ships and cargoes on the high seas have formed themselves into the Lloyd's Society. The system has not changed. It is not an ordinary insurance company but a society of individuals who, having been admitted as members, are prepared to contribute, with fellow members, compensation for loss. The person seeking assurance contacts a broker. The broker submits the proposition to members, who nowadays act as syndicates, each syndicate employing an agent. The broker's proposition passes round the agents, each initialling and 'underwriting' it with the amount his syndicate is prepared to risk, until the whole amount has been underwritten.

In 1774 Lloyd's moved back to the Royal Exchange, and it is still there, and the Stock Exchange is still at Jonathan's Coffee-House in Change Alley.

Newspapers are available and avidly read in the coffee-houses. During this century, many daily newspapers have begun publication – the *Daily Courant* in 1702, the *Evening Post* in 1706, the *London Journal* in 1723 and *The Craftsman* in 1727. Within the next forty years the *Daily Advertiser*, the *Westminster Journal, Lloyd's Evening Post*, the *St James's Chronicle*, the *Middlesex Journal* and the *Morning Chronicle* were launched. In 1771, after the editors and publishers of eight London newspapers had been called to the bar of the House of Commons, the London press, supported by the City, won the right to publish Parliamentary proceedings and debates, and after that time the *Morning Post* appeared in 1780, *The Times* in 1785 and the *Sunday Observer* in 1791.

The Chapter Coffee-House in Paternoster Row, hidden away at the corner of Chapter House Court, is the meeting-place for booksellers and is well known today for 'its punch, its pamphlets and its newspapers'. A recent visitor to London said that, 'Near the Change is a shop where for a penny or even an halfpenny only you may read as many newspapers as you will. There are always a number of people about these shops, who run over the papers as they stand, pay their halfpence and then go on.'

Dr Johnson was a great club man. 'Sir,' he pronounced one day, 'the great chair of a full and pleasant club is, perhaps, the throne of human felicity.' And the essayist Joseph Addison, who was once described as 'the King of Clubs', said that, 'All celebrated clubs are founded on eating and drinking, which are points where most men agree, and in which the learned and illiterate, the dull and the airy, the philosopher and the buffoon, can all of them bear a part. . . . The Kit-Kat is said to have taken its original name from a Mutton-pie. The Beefsteak and October Clubs are neither of them averse to eating and drinking, if we may form a judgment of them from their respective titles.'

The Kit-Kat was the Whig club founded in 1700 by Jacob Tonson, the bookseller and publisher, which met at the shop of a pastry-cook named Christopher Kat, who made a particularly good mutton pie. Its members were dedicated to putting an end to any chance of the Stuart succession after the death of Queen Anne in 1714, and it was not disbanded until the accession of George II, when the Protestant succession seemed assured. The Sublime

Society of Beefsteaks, still flourishes. It was established by John Rich at his Covent Garden theatre, after a friend had found him grilling a steak for his supper in his private room at the theatre, and Rich invited him to join him, together with Lambert, the scene painter. Hogarth was one of the early members, and over the years the company has included Sheridan, Garrick, the Prince of Wales and the Dukes of York and Sussex, all of them enjoying a hearty English dinner with hearty English appetites. After Rich's death, the club was moved to another room at the theatre, and is now at the Shakespeare's Head in Russell Street, where they meet every Saturday night throughout the summer months.

Around St James's and Pall Mall some of the coffee-houses have gradually developed into clubs more exclusive than those further east.

White's, which began as White's Chocolate-House and opened in 1693, is on the east side of St James's Street. By 1723 it had become the great stronghold of the Tory party, with 500 members, all wealthy and aristocratic and fulfilling, in social status, the standard deemed necessary for admission to the club. It is by far the most difficult of all the clubs to enter and does not permit the admission of 'tradesmen', as some of its members regard bankers

A meeting of unfortunate citizens: Charles James Fox outside Brooks's Club in 1798, after his dismissal from the Privy Council

and merchants. There is heavy gambling at White's, the game being whist, and many fortunes are lost. General Scott is one of the lucky ones: he drinks very little when he is about to play, so his brain is not as muddled as those of most of his opponents. He also has a remarkable memory and a profound knowledge of the game, so that he is able to claim that he has won, with honesty, no less than £200,000.

Brooks's Club, opened in St James's Street in 1777, is the venue of the Whig aristocracy and was first initiated at Almack's, a club and assembly rooms in Pall Mall where Charles James Fox, the Duke of Portland and other leading Whigs formed their club, which soon became renowned for its high play. Membership is limited to 450 and is a passport to the Prince of Wales' Carlton House and to Devonshire House.

There is even heavier gambling at Brooks's than at White's. Faro and macao are the two popular games, and Fox and his Whig friends often stay at the table until dawn. Thousands of pounds have been lost in a single night's play – but when Lord Spencer won £100,000, he calmly pocketed the money and has never gambled again.

Charles James Fox is the most reckless gambler of them all, and has lost a fortune. He is nearly always in money trouble, despite the generosity of his father, but it never seems to have affected his untiring work for the Whigs or his genial, friendly manner, despite his political disappointments. This year he is back in Parliament, having absented himself for the last three years, after his dismissal from the Privy Council.

Boodle's Club was not established until some years after Brooks's. There is not much gambling there, and it is not associated with any political party. It is mostly used by elderly country gentlemen, but it is exclusive and has quickly become known for its comfort and excellent food. The author and historian Edward Gibbon, who died six years ago, was one of its distinguished members. Another was the Earl of Westmorland, who was an exceptionally thin man, but with an enormous appetite. The story goes that another member, Michael Taylor, seeing the Earl finishing a roast fowl and a leg of mutton at Boodle's, remarked, 'Well, my lord, I can't make out where you have stowed away your dinner, for I can see no trace of your ever having dined in your lean body.'

'I have finished both, and could now go on for another helping,' replied Lord Westmorland – which says much for Boodle's cooking and for Addison's contention that, 'All celebrated clubs are founded on eating and drinking.'

5. London's Markets

Britain is at war again. Revolutionary France declared war in 1793, and the struggle still goes on.

Inevitably there has been suffering, particularly amongst the poor, as the price of food has risen. For London's trade there have been periods of uncertainty and fluctuation, when French vessels have appeared in the Channel, ready to attack British merchant vessels. On land there have been losses as well as victories. Now the Prime Minister has had to borrow heavily from the City of London, to carry on the war, and this has resulted in a number of bankruptcies. Three years ago there was a mutiny in the Navy against the appalling conditions below decks. There have been riots in the provinces, demanding an end to the war, but those with most to lose insist that it must go on.

In France the young Napoleon Bonaparte is fast rising to power. Nelson's outstanding victory of the Nile two years ago checked him for a time, but he returned secretly from Alexandria to France and is now preparing once more to invade Britain.

There are some who feel that, since the loss of America, Britain has begun to decline in power and prosperity. Two years ago, Colonel George Hanger wrote: 'When first I trod the paths of pleasure in this gay town, my country was arrived at the very height of national grandeur, and was not yet on the decline. She was powerful and respected all over the world; both her fleets and armies were victorious wherever they went; the country was rich, from many years' peace, after a glorious seven years' war. It was then that Great Britain, in the hour of her insolence, drew the jealousy and vengeance of the European powers. There was abundance in every part; the necessaries of life were at a moderate price; the people were happy, joyful and contented; the middle men then lived well; the nobility and gentlemen were in general in a state of opulence; and there was scarcely a thing to be seen in the land as a poor gentleman.'

In fact, the war has had little effect on the social lives of the aristocrats who govern the country, or on the overall trade of the

71

City of London, for the British Navy's command of the seas has not been impaired and the volume of London's trade has continued its steady increase. In addition to the foreign trade which Britain has won from Continental markets, the City now possesses a third of the whole trade of the British Empire. In 1792 the value of London's imports was £19,659,358 and of her exports £24,905,290 and this year imports have risen to £30,570,605 and exports to £43,152,019.

There are three kinds of market in London. First, there are the ancient produce markets – Billingsgate, Leadenhall, Smithfield and Spitalfields, as well as Covent Garden, which is just to the west of the City boundary. Here goods are on display and can be bought on the spot and carried away. Then there are the commodity markets, mostly transacted by the old trading companies, such as the East India Company, where only samples are inspected before sale. Finally there are markets where goods can be bought in advance, before they have even arrived in Britain.

London's oldest produce market is Billingsgate, the fish market, which has been in existence for 800 years. It is situated on the riverside, overlooking the Pool of London, by the City's oldest quay in Thames Street, and is close to Wren's City monument. As soon as you reach the Monument,

> The din and the cries and commotion of the distant market begin to break on the ear like the buzzing of a hornet's nest [wrote a recent visitor to London]. The whole neighbourhood is covered with hand barrows, some laden with baskets, others with sacks. The air is filled with a sea-weedy odour, reminding one of the sea-shore; and on entering the market, the smell of whelks, red herrings, sprats and a hundred other sorts of fish is almost overpowering. The wooden, barn-looking square where the fish is sold is, soon after six o'clock, crowded with shiny cord jackets and greasy caps. Everybody comes to Billingsgate in his worst clothes; and no one knows the length of time a coat can be worn until they have been to a fish sale. . . . Over the hum of voices is heard the shouts of the salesmen, who, with their white aprons, peering above the heads of the mob, stand on their tables roaring out their prices. All are bawling together – salesmen and hucksters . . . till the place is a perfect babel of competition.

Mr Goldham, the clerk of the market, has recently stated before a Parliamentary Committee that 400 fishermen, each of whom is the owner of a boat and employs a boy, obtain a good livelihood by the exercise of their craft between Deptford and London, above and below the bridge, taking roach, plaice, smelts, flounders, salmon,

A Billingsgate fishwife

shad, eels, gudgeon, dace and dabs. He said that no fewer than 3,000 Thames salmon were brought to Billingsgate during the season, selling at 3 to 4 shillings a pound, the boats sometimes making as much as £6 a week.

Billingsgate began as a small general market, but very soon, because of the plentiful supply in the Thames, its most important commodity became fish. In Tudor times the fishing industry was given every protection and encouragement, for it was from experienced fishermen that the sailors of the Royal Navy were recruited in time of war. After the Reformation, meatless days were no longer enforced in England for religious reasons – in fact, it was declared illegal for anyone to insist that it was a religious duty to fast. However, in order to protect the fishing industry and maintain a supply of skilled seamen for the Navy, it was decreed that fish must be eaten on Fridays during Lent, and there were fines and penalties for anyone who broke the law. After 1563 Wednesdays were also declared fast days, so that England then had more meatless days than any other country in Europe. These Fishing Acts created so much extra demand for fish that a thousand more men were brought into the industry, all of whom, said the report, would be available and 'ready to serve in Her Majesty's ships'.

Half of England's fish supply came from the Thames. 'What should I speak of the fat and sweet salmon daily taken in this stream,' wrote the sixteenth-century Londoner John Stow, 'and that in such plenty (after the time of the smelt is past) as no river in Europe is able to exceed it? But what store also of barbels, trouts, chevens, perches, smelts, breams, roaches, daces, gudgeons, flounders, shrimps, eels etc. are commonly to be had therein. . . .' In addition to these supplies, fish caught in the Thames estuary and the North Sea were also brought to Billingsgate, for sale to Londoners.

As fish became an increasingly important item of food, so did the importance of Billingsgate as a fish market. By the end of the seventeenth century it dealt almost entirely in fish, and an Act of Parliament made Billingsgate 'a free and open market for all sorts of fish whatsoever, six days of the week, and on Sundays (before Divine Service) for mackerel'; any fishmonger who bought, except for his own sale, was to be sentenced to a fine of £20 for every offence.

Today, with the shortage of bread caused by the war with France, the Government is again urging people to eat more fish.

Water transport is used wherever possible to carry the fish from London, and within recent years the development of the canals has

Billingsgate

helped, but carrier carts will take Billingsgate fish about twenty-five miles inland, to such places as Windsor, St Albans, Hertford and Romford, and deliver it still fresh. About fifteen years ago a member of the East India Company told a friend in Scotland of the Chinese fishermen's way of sending fresh fish long distances packed in ice, and this friend has tried the method successfully, sending salmon from Aberdeen and Inverness to London.

Fishery laws have been passed to restrain some of the abuses among fishermen, such as blowing up cod with pipes to make them look bigger and mixing dead eels in with a consignment of live ones. In 1760 an Act was passed to regulate the sale of fish and prevent a monopoly of the market, for some fishermen were keeping the fish down at Gravesend and supplying the market with only single boatloads at a time, in order to keep up the price. Now the master of every laden fishing boat arriving at the Nore has to report the time of his arrival, and the cargo he brings, to the clerk of the coast office, under penalty of £20, and for any marketable fish he destroys he is liable to be sentenced to a month's hard labour.

The middlemen at Billingsgate are the 'bummarees'. They buy the unsold fish and sell it again, in lots, to fishmongers and costermongers. They derive their name from the bumboat-men who buy from the wind-bound smacks at Gravesend or the Nore and get the fish quickly up to the market in light carts. The costermongers are important people in Billingsgate, for they now buy a third of the entire fish sent there for re-sale in the streets.

The market opens at four o'clock in the morning. For the first two or three hours the sale is to the regular fishmongers and bummarees; as soon as they have gone, the costers move in to buy the remainder.

Billingsgate is also the embarkation point for passengers to Gravesend and other places down river, and as the boats have to wait for the tides, the passengers often arrive at strange hours, which means that there must be plenty of taverns for their accommodation. This – particularly among the costers, both men and women – leads to too much drinking and the resultant ribald language. Ned Ward, the writer, who in 1706 published *The Wealthy Shopkeeper*, called the shrill-voiced, half-drunk fishwives, scolding and chattering among their heaps of fish, 'a screaming, fighting, half-tipsy crowd, ready enough to knock down the auctioneer who did not knock down a lot to them' as they bargained in the dirty, fishy market sheds. In fact, in Bailey's dictionary, published in 1735, 'a Billingsgate' is defined as 'a scolding, impudent slut', a far cry from the accepted origin of the name, for Billingsgate is said to have derived from the Celtic King Belin, who was ruling here about 400 BC, when the Celtic settlement consisted of a few mud huts surrounded by an earth wall, called Llyn-Din, the Hill by the Pool. Belin ordered that a small landing place be cut along the river front, with a wooden quay, and to enter the settlement from the quayside, a watergate was made in the wall, called Belingsgate.

Leadenhall Market, in Leadenhall Street, only a short walk from Billingsgate up Gracechurch Street, is the place for poultry and game.

Early in the fourteenth century, a mansion stood here in large grounds. The roof of the house was lined with lead, which in those days of plaster and timber dwellings was a remarkable innovation, and it was this feature which gave it the curious name of Leaden Hall. The owner was Sir Hugh Neville, and he gave permission for a market to be held in the grounds, for the benefit of his tenants.

The market proved so successful that a hundred years later, when Sir Richard Whittington was mayor of London, the City Corporation acquired the site and became lords of the manor of Leadenhall.

A few years later, in 1445, after a series of bad harvests, the mayor of that year, Sir Simon Eyre, converted the mansion into a large granary, where grain could be stored, so that, in the event of a similar shortage in future years, the City would have a supply on which to draw. The rest of the space was an open market, where meat, fish, poultry and vegetables were sold, as well as hides, wool, woollen cloth and metal goods. Foreign visitors often marvelled at the bountiful supplies of food displayed at Leadenhall, and when the Spanish Ambassador visited the market with Charles II, he told the King he believed there was more meat sold in that market than in all the kingdom of Spain in a whole year.

The market was partly rebuilt in 1730 but has changed very little since then, except that it is specializing more and more in excellent poultry and game.

Smithfield, the market for live cattle, lies in the north-west corner of the City, between Charterhouse Street and Aldersgate, and it covers three acres. Monday is the day for fat cattle and sheep; Tuesday, Thursday and Saturday mornings are for the sale of hay and straw, and the afternoons for horses and donkeys; on Fridays cattle, sheep and milch cows are on sale.

A large number of these animals are slaughtered in West Smithfield, and the meat is sold to the butchers of Newgate Street close by, on the other side of St Bartholomew's hospital. But as ever more buildings crowd round this corner of the City, it has become increasingly unsuitable for a cattle market. Conditions for the animals are appalling, and they obviously suffer.

Smithfield is in fact no pleasanter a place than Billingsgate. Newgate market, where the meat is sold, is no better, as it is both a retail market and the place where meat arrives from all over the country. All this business is crowded into far too small an area. 'Through the filthy lanes and alleys no one can pass without being either butted with the dripping end of a quarter of beef, or smeared with a greasy carcase of a newly slain sheep. In many of the narrow lanes there is hardly room for two persons to pass abreast,' wrote another visitor recently. Yet there seem to be no plans at the moment to improve matters.

For all its present squalor, Smithfield, like Billingsgate, stands on historic ground, for cattle have been bought and sold here since early medieval times. On the south side of the market, in West Smithfield, is St Bartholomew's hospital, which was founded in 1123 by Rahere, a canon of St Paul's Cathedral, and also his beautiful Norman church of St Bartholomew the Great.

The cartoonist's view of one of the miseries of human life: 'As you are quietly walking along in the vicinity of Smithfield on Market day finding yourself suddenly obliged though your dancing days have been long over, to lead outsides, cross over, foot it, and a variety of other steps and figures, – with mad bulls for your partners.'

Smithfield was once known as 'the smooth field'. It was just outside the City walls, but within its jurisdiction. A horse fair was held here every Friday and on other days of the week horses, cattle, sheep and pigs were bought and sold – it was also known as the King's market. When Rahere planned his hospital for the poor citizens of London, and his adjacent priory, King Henry I granted him the site of the King's market, with its valuable market tolls.

Pilgrims used to visit the priory, particularly during the times of Church festivals. Hucksters and vendors of all kinds always appeared on these occasions, and Smithfield began to take on the appearance of a fairground, which is how St Bartholomew's Fair began. In the early days, it was mainly a cloth fair, and drapers and clothiers used to keep their wares inside the priory walls for safety. The priors of St Bartholomew were the Lords of the Fair and received the fair tolls, but after the Reformation the City Fathers stepped in and claimed this income. The weekly horse market was still held, but on other days Smithfield was used for tournaments and archery contests – and the annual fair.

During the reign of Charles I, the City of London finally took full control of Smithfield and organized it as the market for live cattle which it is today. But the Fair still goes on, each year growing rowdier, the people more drunk, the place muddier and more dangerous. When Ned Ward the writer and journalist, visited the Fair as the 'London Spy', he took a coach, to escape the dirt and the crowd. He was '. . . saluted with Belphegor's concert, the rumbling of drums, mixed with the intolerable squeaking of cat-calls and penny trumpets, made more terrible with the shrill belches of lottery pickpockets through instruments of the same metal with their faces'. From the windows of a tavern he looked down on a crowd 'rushing and ankle deep in filth, through an air tainted by the fumes of tobacco and of singeing, over-roasted pork, to see the Merry Andrew'.

'There are rope-dancers who gett their living merely by hazarding their lives,' wrote Sir Robert Southwell to his son, 'and why men will pay money and make pleasure to see such danger, is of separate and philosophical consideration. You have others who are acting fools, drunkards and madmen, but for the same wages which they might get by honest labour, and live with credit besides. Others, if born in any monstrous shape, or have children that are such, forget how odious they are made. . . . 'Tis out of this credulous crowd that the ballad-singers attackt an assembly, who listen and admire, while their confederate pickpockets are diving and fishing for prey.'

Last year Rowlandson made some of his satirical drawings of the Fair: the sickening boat-swings, the exhibition of unfortunates born with physical abnormalities, the weight-lifters, the pickpockets, the crowds of rough and boisterous sightseers, the sink for all the vices of London. But still the Fair goes on, and the number of cases of felony, misdemeanour and assault committed there, which are heard at the Guildhall and duly punished, increases every year.

Spitalfields market lies hidden away behind Bishopsgate, only a few yards to the east, down Brushfield Street. This area is just beyond the old city boundary and the bishop's gate which once guarded its eastern approaches. It is today an important market for home-grown fruit, vegetables, meat and poultry, which are brought in from country districts outlying the parishes of Spitalfields, Shoreditch and Bethnal Green.

Spitalfields has an interesting history. In the twelfth century the London aldermen who owned the fields offered them for the site of a priory and hospital, and a silk mercer paid for the building. The hospital was dedicated to the Virgin Mary and named St Mary Spital (hospital) and it did valuable work for the next three or four centuries. By the time of the Reformation, the hospital had 180 beds, but it was pulled down, together with the priory. However, the hospital churchyard remained, and with it the pulpit of Spital Cross, from which sermons were preached each year during Easter week. There was a small building opposite the pulpit, where the Lord Mayor, aldermen and sheriffs, dressed in the full panoply of their office, always came to hear the sermons, their ladies sitting at a window on the first floor; and there was another building close by for the governor and children of Christ's Hospital. During the Civil War the pulpit was destroyed, but until the Great Fire the Spital sermons continued, being preached in St Paul's Cathedral, and now at Christ Church, Newgate Street.

On the site of the hospital a few large houses were built round a square field known as Spital Square, and in 1682 a silk thrower, John Balch, applied for permission to hold a market there twice a week. Three years later, when hundreds of Protestants fled from France, a number came to England. Among these Huguenots were many skilled weavers, who settled in Spitalfields to earn their living. Cottages were built for them, elegant little buildings with intricate fanlights over the pedimented front doors, beautifully carved staircases, ornamental plaster ceilings and wide, latticed windows in the upper storeys, to give extra light for their looms.

The French weavers' skill was incomparable and they produced materials vastly superior to anything London had seen before. The silk weaving of Spitalfields became a flourishing industry, and the population of the area rapidly increased, so that very soon there was a network of lanes and alleyways covering the fields which had once surrounded the Spital.

There are 500 master weavers living in the Spital Square now, and 50,000 people in the area are dependent on the industry, with about 15,000 looms at work. Thousands of yards of expensive velvet and silk are sent from here all over the world. The weavers work fourteen to sixteen hours a day on very poor pay. Most are now British, but the master weavers are still of French extraction, tracing their ancestry back to the refugees of 1685. However, with the invention of the power loom, which is now being used in many other parts of the country, it looks as though the hand weaver's trade may not last much longer.

As the population of Spitalfields has increased, so has the market. The thrifty Huguenots introduced to Londoners, amongst many other things, the art of making ox-tail soup. Previously the market butchers had thrown away the tails, but the weavers, who are excellent cooks, put them to good use. They are nearly all bird-fanciers, too, and supply London with half its singing birds – linnets, woodlarks, goldfinches and greenfinches, all of which are sold here.

There was a covered market building in the square at one time, but some years ago it was burned down and has never been replaced, so business is now transacted in its three acres of open stalls and sheds.

Covent Garden, lying just north of the Strand, is the largest and most important fruit and vegetable market not only in London but in the whole country, but today it is in need of drastic re-organization.

The abbots of Westminster once owned this seven acres of 'fair, spreading pasture' – their Convent Garden and the Long Acre – which they had used partly as a burial ground and partly as an orchard and vegetable garden for their daily needs. The surplus they marketed to the surrounding villages. At the Reformation, the land was granted to John Russell, Earl of Bedford. The Russells did little with it at first, but their gardeners tended the garden, and the informal market, soon to be known as 'Covent' Garden, continued. Then, facing the Strand, the Russells built Bedford House, and in the middle of the seventeenth century, as the population of London increased and the demand for houses grew, they commissioned Inigo Jones to lay out the square, surrounded by noble mansions, and to plan four streets to converge on it, with a small church at the western end.

Inigo Jones built his beautiful square and piazza in the Palladian tradition, and the houses quickly became the height of fashion, the homes of the wealthy aristocrats who no longer wished to live in the City. Although the market did not move, but remained to serve the needs of its increasing number of customers, it was restricted to a narrow space behind the garden wall of Bedford House. But now Inigo Jones's creation, which was so much admired and welcomed, has been ruined.

It was in 1670 that Charles II granted the Russell family a charter for their market. Twenty-three salesmen were registered, licensed to sell flowers, fruit and vegetables every day of the week except Sundays and Christmas Day. They also gained permission to build cellars and shops along the outside of the garden wall of Bedford House, which faced onto the Strand, but there were to be no chimneys, and the shops were to have a uniform frontage, one foot

Fun and games at Bartholomew Fair, by Rowlandson

A general fast in consequence of the war as observed in Lambeth (left) and Spitalfields

lower than the Bedford House garden wall, and not more than eight feet wide. The market people were '. . . to sit in order between the rails and the garden wall, from one to the other thereof', thereby keeping well away from the centre of the square, which was a fashionable and pleasant promenade, in the middle of which was a tall column, mounted on six marble steps and supporting a large, square stone, on three sides of which were sun dials.

The streets around the square were all very narrow, and traffic soon became a serious problem, for there was a congestion of sedan chairs and coaches, going to and from the theatres, mixing incongruously with the carts laden with market produce. But still the market grew. Spitalfields market was as yet small and local. The Stocks market, which had been moved from the City to make way for the building of the Mansion House, was opened in Farringdon Street, but it did not prosper in the same way, the Surrey and Kent growers preferring to bring their produce to Covent Garden. The residents at last protested, lodging a complaint with the Duke of Bedford against the nuisance and inconvenience the traffic was causing and begging him to '. . . take the favourable occasion that will soon offer, by the expiration of the lease of the market, to become the happy instrument of reviving the decaying credit of the parish and restoring it to its pristine flourishing state. . . .' However, the Duke ignored the petition and renewed the lease of the market, and as it continued to spread, the sorely tried residents gradually moved away.

When the ducal family left Bedford House for their new mansion in Bloomsbury, the market was still confined mainly to the stalls and sheds along the garden wall, but when, a little later, Bedford House and its garden walls were demolished, to make way for the building of Tavistock Street and Southampton Street, the market began to spread into the piazza. Then salesmen began to build sleeping accommodation for themselves among the sheds and booths. On the elegant marble steps of the central column of the square old women sat, selling bowls of porridge and milk.

As the market spread relentlessly and the residents again protested in vain, they too moved away – and this time their houses were deserted. Some were soon being let out in apartments, others became gaming houses or brothels. Now some have been taken over by the market people, but others by disreputable members of London's underworld, who have let them fall into a state of almost irremediable decay.

Covent Garden today is a sad sight. Even the central column has now been removed, the last sign of its former elegance. Diprose has described '. . . the turbulent and drunken old women, the porters quarrelling over their morning potations . . . the London rakes – making not the night but the morning hideous by their obscene blasphemies, and deeming it conduct becoming of gentlemen to interrupt honest industry and to scoff at early labour. . . .'

'People who know Covent Garden only in its quiet afternoon aspect,' says a writer in the *City Press*, 'can form no idea of the vile den it is at the busy hour of daybreak. . . . We are fully cognisant of the fact that Spitalfields and Farringdon absorb some portion of the trade in vegetables; but Covent Garden is *the* market *par excellence*, and it is a disgrace to the metropolis to be compelled to rely on the capabilities of a place which, spacious as it may be, is fitted at the very utmost to serve as a market for a town of 60,000 inhabitants.'

It surely cannot be long before the Russells do something to improve matters.

Britain's present prosperity, despite the war with France, is due to the enormous expansion of her colonies and overseas possessions. Her overseas trade is carried on mainly through companies

And when the show is over, and all the Gain we've got
Why then our Brother Alderman Alas, he goes to Pot
Hey down he down derry derry down O the Corporation
Hogs of Windsor.

Cruikshank's opinion of the new Lord Mayor: 'The Corporation's visit to their brother in Smithfield or the Hog's Feast on being sworn in.'

founded in the sixteenth century – such as the East India Company and Hudson's Bay Company. Recently the *British Directory* proclaimed: 'By the spirited exertions of the City of London, seconded by the merchants of the principal trading towns in the country, the rental of England is now estimated at twenty millions per annum or more: of which vast benefit our nobility, gentry, and landholders begin to be fully sensible, by the immense increase in the value or fee-simple of their lands, which has gradually kept pace with the increase and value of our commercial intercourse with foreign nations.'

These are Britain's current markets:

To Turkey are exported woollen cloths, tin, lead and iron in our own shipping; from Turkey come raw silk, carpets, dyeing ingredients, cotton, fruit and medicinal drugs.

To Italy are exported woollen goods, peltry, leather, lead, tin, fish and East India merchandise; from Italy come raw and thrown silk, wines, oil, soap, olives, oranges, lemons, pomegranates, dried fruits and anchovies.

To Spain are sent woollen goods, leather, lead, tin, iron and brass manufactures, fish, corn, haberdashery and assortment of linen from Germany and elsewhere for her American colonies; from Spain are imported wines, oils, dried fruit, oranges, lemons, olives, indigo, cochineal and other dyeing drugs, gold and silver coins. To Portugal Britain's exports are the same as those to Spain, and imports include wines, oils, salt, dried and moist fruits, dyers' ingredients and gold coins.

To France, when not at war with Britain, are exported tobacco, lead, tin, flannels, hardware, Manchester goods and sometimes large quantities of corn, and wines, brandies, linens, cambricks, lace, velvet and brocades are imported. To Flanders are sent serges, flannels, tin, lead, sugar and tobacco, receiving fine lace, linen and cambricks.

To Germany Britain exports cloth, tin, pewter, sugar, tobacco and East India merchandise, and from Germany come linen, thread, goatskins, tinned plates, timber and wine.

Britain exports tobacco and woollen stuffs to Norway and imports deal and other timbers. Sweden takes most of our home manufactures and exports iron, copper, timber and tar.

To Russia are exported woollen cloths, tin, lead, tobacco, diamonds and household furniture, and Russia sends hemp, flax, linen, thread, furs, potash, iron, wax and tallow.

To Holland are sent woollen goods, hides, corn and coal, as well as already imported East India and Turkey goods and tobacco, tar, sugar, rice and ginger which have come from America; Holland sends in return fine linen, lace, cambricks, thread, tapes, madder, drugs, whalebone and numerous small articles, including toys.

America still accepts home manufactures of almost every kind, and exports tobacco, sugar, rice, ginger, indigo, drugs, logwood and timber.

To the Guinea coast are sent woollen and linen goods, iron, pewter, brass and hardware manufactures, lead shot, swords, knives, firearms, gunpowder and glass manufactures, importing by way of payment Negro slaves, gold dust, dyeing and medicinal drugs, redwood, Guinea grains and ivory.

According to the *Annual Register* of 1789, which published points made by William Wilberforce in his attempt to have the slave trade abolished (which he failed to carry), the number of slaves carried annually from the coast of Africa in British ships is about 38,000. Those taken to the British West India Islands average 22,500. Those who stay in Britain average 17,500. In that year the number of slaves in Jamaica was 256,000, and in Barbados 62,000.

Many London merchants are sincerely sympathetic to the plight of the Negroes and would be prepared to see the trade abolished, but in the midst of war and with the threat of Bonaparte's invasion, they feel that other matters are more urgent.

Continuing the list of countries with whom Britain trades, we must include Ireland, Newfoundland, the West Indies and many other settlements throughout the world, which also contribute large annual returns. To Arabia, Persia, the East Indies and China Britain sends foreign silver coin and bullion, as well as manufactures of lead, iron, brass and woollen goods, bringing back muslins, cottons of various kinds, calicoes, raw and wrought silk, chintz, tea, coffee, porcelain, gold-dust, saltpetre and drugs for dyers and medicinal uses.

Since the heavy import duty on tea ended sixteen years ago, the windjammers (merchant sailing ships) of the East India Company are bringing their tea from China by way of the Cape of Good Hope, in increasing quantities. It is stored in the Company's dockside warehouses in London, and samples are brought to the East India House in Leadenhall Street, where the tea is sold by auction in the General Court Room. So far the Company has no rivals, but there are signs that America will soon be in the race, and her clippers are much faster than the Company's old windjammers.

The import of foreign wool is forbidden, in order to protect the British market, and the trade in wool is based in Leadenhall market.

Furs have been traded in London for centuries, but it was when English adventurers discovered the furs of Canada that London became the centre of the world fur trade. King Charles II granted a charter to the English fur-trading company that was formed, and Prince Rupert was its first governor, the company being given powers to operate the vast territory comprising all the rivers which drain into Hudson Bay. It was called 'The Company of Adventurers of England Trading into Hudson Bay', and its first meetings were held in Prince Rupert's private quarters in the Tower of London. Soon the merchants had so many furs that they hardly knew how to dispose of them. Some they sold privately. Others were sent to the fur-dealers of Leipzig, Amsterdam, Paris and Vienna. But the quality and quantity of the furs reaching London was so high that European dealers were soon coming to London to buy. The first public auction of Hudson Bay furs took place in 1671, at Mr Garraway's coffee-house in Change Alley, off Cornhill. There was a large variety of furs on offer, including beaver skins, which were immensely popular – men are still wearing beaver hats today.

Hamilton Place, off Piccadilly

When the company outgrew Garraway's, they moved to their present sale-room in Fenchurch Street.

The various corn markets in London gradually concentrated on two main areas. The first was Whitechapel, where Essex farmers bringing their corn to London used to meet. As business increased, they began to leave samples of their crops with the landlord of the inn which had become their meeting-place, and he took orders from the bakers and brewers who came to inspect them, passed them back to the farmers and received a commission on the sale.

Down in Thames Street, where the grain ships from the Baltic discharged their cargoes, was Jack's Coffee-House, which, in the same way, became a market for imported corn. Corn merchants who acted as brokers would buy cargoes in bulk and sell them to the bakers and brewers.

In 1747 the large Corn Exchange was built in Mark Lane, which today houses both the growing business of the Whitechapel market and that of Jack's Coffee-House.

The Virginia and Maryland Coffee-House in Threadneedle Street was the meeting-place for merchants interested in the tobacco, sugar and cotton of the southern states of America, and close by was the Baltic, where men dealing in the Russian and

89

Baltic trade in timber and tallow did business. In 1744 the Virginia and Maryland joined forces with the Baltic and re-opened as the Virginia and Baltic. By then their customers were as interested in the ships as in their cargoes and met the owners and captains in order to check their movements and the amount of cargo space they had available at any given time. For example, a merchant wishing to send tea and coffee he had bought from the East India Company to customers in America might arrange with a captain bringing tallow and grain from the Baltic to reload his ship in London with the tea and coffee and advise the American customer to have ready a cargo of sugar and tobacco which the ship could carry on the return journey to Europe, thereby saving both time and money. In this way the 'shipping market' of the Baltic was established, which soon became as important as the commodity markets.

When plans for rebuilding the London docks, now under way, are completed, they will be infinitely more efficient. At present, the big, cargo-laden ships come no higher than London Bridge, and the Pool is covered with a forest of masts which amaze foreign visitors. Their cargoes have to be unloaded by scores of lighters, barges, punts and luggerboats, employing hundreds of labourers.

6. Shops and Shopping

London has the finest shops in Europe. The poet Shelley, writing this year to Thomas Manning, said: 'Oh, the lamps of a night! her rich goldsmiths, print-shops, toy-shops, mercers, hardware men, pastry-cooks, St Paul's Churchyard, the Strand, Exeter Change, Charing Cross, with a man upon a black horse! These are thy gods, O London!'

A recent visitor has described how the shops are spread through the city:

> There are two sets of streets, running nearly parallel, almost from the Eastern extremity of the town to the Western, forming (with the exception of a very few houses), a line of shops. One, lying to the south, nearer the river, extends from Mile End to Parliament Street, including Whitechapel, Leadenhall Street, Cornhill, Cheapside, St Paul's Churchyard, Ludgate Hill, Fleet Street, the Strand and Charing Cross. The other, to the north, reaches from Shoreditch Church almost to the end of Oxford Street, including Shoreditch, Bishopsgate Street, Threadneedle Street, Cheapside, Newgate Street, Snow Hill, Broad Street, St Giles and Oxford Street.
>
> The southern line, which is the most splendid, is more than three miles in length; the other is about four miles. There are several large streets also occupied by the retail trade, that run parallel to parts of the two grand lines, or intersect them, among the most remarkable of which are Fenchurch Street and Gracechurch Street in the City of London; and Cockspur Street, Pall Mall, St James's Street, Piccadilly, King Street, Covent Garden, and New Bond Street, at the west end of the town.

In most of these shops, the proprietor-shopkeeper lives with his family above or behind his business premises. He is more than a man who handles merchandise: he is a specialist in the goods he sells, and very often the craftsman who makes them – whether he be shoemaker, tailor, staymaker, hatter, fan-maker, umbrella-maker or jeweller – there is no clear division between retailer and wholesaler.

There are no regular shopping hours. The shopkeeper opens his shop before breakfast, and it stays open until he goes to bed.

The streetlighting in London is by the very dim, oil-burning parish lamps, but enterprising shopkeepers provide lamps of their own, to shine onto their goods, which is particularly useful during the long, dark winter evenings.

In the southern line of shops on Cornhill, there have been drapers for centuries. Today, among the taverns and coffee-houses, there are drapers, peruke-makers (wig-makers) and per-fumiers, and at number 15 is the shop of Birch, the renowned cook and confectioner.

At 108 Cheapside, opposite Bow Church, is the shop of David Barclay, the linen draper, which has been visited by six reigning sovereigns, from Charles II to the present King, George III, during various civic festivities, and also because it is an excellent place for watching the Lord Mayor's procession.

Number 90 is the printshop of Alderman Boydell. There were few printshops in London before he opened his business, and very few prints were made, such as existed being imported from France. But Boydell, who was apprenticed to an engraver, was an enthu-siast. He paid the best engravers he could find to make copies of great masterpieces. Then he began to form his collection of modern historical pictures. He employed artists, including Fuseli and Sir Joshua Reynolds, to paint the pictures, and then engravers to make the prints from them. For his first collection, the subjects were taken from Shakespeare's plays, and it was called 'The Shakespeare Gallery'.

Alderman Boydell has established a school of engravers in London and completely transformed the engraving business, so that today very few prints are imported and the foreign market is principally supplied with prints from London. A very old man now and in failing health, he has spent more than £350,000 in promoting the art of engraving, giving much valued work to both artists and engravers, but he is now obliged to sell, by lottery, some of the paintings and drawings he has commissioned over the years, in order to pay his increasing debts.

In St Paul's churchyard are many booksellers and publishers. At number 65 is John Newbery's business. He was the friend and employer of the novelist and playwright Oliver Goldsmith. His nephew published Goldsmith's *The Vicar of Wakefield*, and New-bery himself *The Traveller*. Goldsmith also wrote for Newbery's daily newspaper *The Public Ledger*, which first appeared forty years ago. Although he was living in prosperous London and was so gifted, Goldsmith was always in financial troubles. When a friend he happened to meet in the street gave him some money, after he had admitted that he had had nothing to eat for several days, he spent it on new, hot bread, and it killed him. He was only forty-six when he died, in 1774.

Joseph Johnson of number 72 in the churchyard, published William Cowper's first volume of poems and also the Olney hymns which Cowper, who died this year, wrote in collaboration with John Newton, the curate of Olney.

Samuel Taylor Coleridge

Paternoster Row is full of stationers, booksellers and publishers, the most important, and the largest in the City, being the house of Longman. The first Longman in the business was born in 1699 and bought the firm from Mr Taylor, who had published *Robinson Crusoe*. After Longman's death, a nephew succeeded to the business and did a great deal of trade with America. Now his son has inherited the firm and taken Owen Rees as partner. They have recently acquired some new and valuable copyrights, including the work of Wordsworth and Coleridge – the second edition of their *Lyrical Ballads* was published this year.

Ludgate Hill also has publishers and bookshops, as well as some splendid mercers, who include among their wares Dutch ratteens, duffles, friezes, beaver coating, kerseymeres, forrest cloths,

93

German serges, Wilton stuffs, sagathies, nankeen, Silesia cambricks, Manchester velvets, silks, grosgrams, allapeens, double allapeens, silk camblets, barragins, Brussels camblets, princes stuffs, worsted damasks, silk knitpieces, corded silks, gattias, shagg velvets, serge desoys and shalloons.

A visitor to London recently described a visit to Ludgate Hill:

This afternoon some ladies, having an opinion of my fancy in clothes, desired me to accompany them to Ludgate-hill, which I take to be as agreeable an amusement as a lady can pass away three or four hours in. The shops are perfect gilded theatres, the variety of wrought silks so many changes of fine scenes, and the mercers are the performers in the opera; and instead of *vivitur ingenio* you have in golden capitals, 'No trust by retail'. They are the sweetest, fairest, nicest, dished-out creatures; and by their elegant address and soft speeches, you would guess them to be Italians. As people glance within their doors, they salute them with – 'Garden-silks, ladies; Italian silks; very fine mantua silks; any right Geneva velvet, English velvet, velvet embossed?' And to the meaner sort – 'Fine thread satins, both stripe and plain; fine mohair silks; satinets; burdets; Perianets; Norwich crapes; anterines; silks for hoods and scarves; hair camlets, druggets, sagathies; gentleman's nightgowns ready-made, shalloons, durances, and right Scotch plaids.'

We went into a shop which had three partners; two of them were to flourish out their silks, and, after an obliging smile and a pretty mouth made Cicero-like, to expatiate on their goodness; and the other's sole business, was to be gentleman usher of the shops, to stand completely dressed at the door, bow to all the coaches that pass by, and hand ladies out and in. We saw abundance of gay fancies, fit for sea-captains' wives, sheriffs' feasts, and Taunton-dean ladies. 'This, madam, is wonderful charming. This madam, is so diverting a silk. This, madam, my stars! how cool it looks! But this, madam – ye Gods! Would I had 10,000 yards of it!' Then gathers up a sleeve, and places it to our shoulders. 'It suits your ladyship's face wonderfully well.' When we had pleased ourselves, and bid him ten shillings a yard for what he asked fifteen: 'Fan me, ye winds, your ladyship rallies me! Should I part with it at such a price, the weavers would rise upon the very shop. Was you at the Park last night, madam? Your ladyship shall abate me sixpence. Have you read the *Tatler* today?'

Perhaps the best-known shop on Ludgate Hill is number 32, the celebrated goldsmiths and diamond merchants, Rundell & Bridge.

Until a few years ago all these shops had their street signs hanging above their bow-fronted windows, but as the signs became larger and larger, as shopkeepers vied with each other to attract attention, they became serious obstructions and very dangerous in windy weather, sometimes causing accidents, so at last the Government forbade them, except for the three balls of the pawnbrokers. All the Turk's heads, plumes of feathers, flaming swords, civet cats, olive trees, three crowns and king's arms came down. A few are now attached to the front wall of the shop, but today the houses and shops are identified by numbers.

Coming down from Ludgate Hill, we reach Fleet Street, the resort of authors, both the successful and the failures. Of Fleet Street, Dr Johnson said:

It is my practice when I am in want of amusement, to place myself for an hour at Temple Bar, or any other narrow pass much frequented, and examine one by one the looks of the passengers, and I have commonly found that between the hours of eleven and four every sixth man is an author. They are seldom to be seen very early in the morning or late in the evening, but about dinner-time they are all in motion, and have one uniform eagerness in their faces, which gives little opportunity of discerning their hopes or fears, their pleasure or their pains.

But in the afternoon, when they have all dined, or composed themselves to pass the day without a dinner, their passions have full play, and I can perceive one man wondering at the stupidity of the public, by which his new book has been totally neglected; another cursing the French, who fright away literary curiosity by their threat of an invasion; another swearing at this bookseller, who will advance no money without 'copy'; another perusing as he walks his publisher's bill; another murmuring at an unanswerable criticism; another determining to write no more to a generation of barbarians; and another wishing to try once again whether he cannot awaken the drowsy world to a sense of his merit.

Among the booksellers of Fleet Street who arouse all these emotions is Bernard Lintot at number 16, the publisher of Pope's *Homer*. At number 32 John Murray opened business in 1768. At his death, in 1793, his son was only fifteen and the business was conducted by Samuel Highley, but now John Murray the second is in full control.

Next to Hoare's bank is the Mitre tavern, where Dr Johnson and Boswell had their first meeting. At number 67, at the corner of Whitefriars Street, is the clock- and watchmaker's shop where Thomas Tompion, the famous watchmaker of Queen Anne's time, opened his business. He is said to have begun the making of a clock for St Paul's Cathedral which would go for a hundred years

Fleet market. The Stocks market was demolished when the Mansion House was built and re-established on ground reclaimed by the covering of the Fleet ditch. Here it was known as the Fleet market

without being wound up, but nothing more has been heard of it. After his death, in 1713, his apprentice George Graham succeeded to the business, and then Mudge & Dutton, who in 1768 made Dr Johnson's first watch.

At number 161 is the shop of Thomas Hardy, the bootmaker. Samuel Richardson's printing office was at the north-west corner of Salisbury Square, communicating with his office at 76 Fleet Street, where he wrote *Pamela*, and here Oliver Goldsmith became his reader. Richardson was a kindly man and is said to have encouraged his workmen to rise early to work by hiding half-crowns in the printing room, so that the earliest comer might find his virtue rewarded. Richardson became printer of the journals of the House of Commons, Master of the Stationers' Company and finally King's Law Printer.

At 127 Fleet Street the *Morning Advertiser* was launched six years ago, to replace the *Daily Advertiser*. It was established by the Society of Licensed Victuallers as a mutual benefit society, every member being obliged to buy the paper and take a share in the profits – any member falling on hard times becomes a pensioner of the institution. The paper is read mainly in the taverns and coffee-houses. From the outset it has been a success, and today its circulation has reached 5,000.

No. 12, Green Arbour Court, off the Old Bailey. Goldsmith had a room here in the 1750s

Number 98 is John Brasbridge's silversmith's shop, which has many distinguished customers, including Lady Hamilton. Number 106 is John Hardham's tobacco shop, and he has grown rich with the manufacture of his 'No. 37 snuff', the ingredients of which he has never revealed.

In the streets leading from Fleet Street there are dozens of small printers and publishers and shops of all kinds, including Whitehead's, the master tailor, and William and John Sangster, the umbrella- and parasol-manufacturers.

In Salisbury Square William Woodfall, editor and printer of the *Morning Chronicle*, has his office. He is often known as 'Memory' Woodfall, for he has the extraordinary ability of being able to report from memory the speeches he hears in the House of Commons. He achieves this through intense concentration, with his eyes closed and his hands clasped on his knees, and he claims that the words of a debate stay in his head for at least a fortnight.

The Strand is another street of taverns, banks and shops. At number 217 is Snow's Bank, and next to it Child's Bank. Opposite Butcher's Row, between the Strand and Devereux Court, are the banking house and adjoining tea warehouse of Thomas Twining. They were established in 1710, when there were very few houses trading in tea and it was costing between 20 and 30 shillings a pound. In those days ladies of fashion would flock to Mr Twining's to sip their tea from tiny china cups, at a shilling a cup, but nowadays nearly everyone can afford Twining's tea.

At 132 Arundel Street Mr Wright established the first circulating library in 1740. He soon had four rivals, in the streets close by, but by 1770 there were only four circulating libraries in the whole of London, so some of these early ventures must have failed.

At number 141 in the Strand is the bookshop of Thomas Cadell, whose publications include Gibbon's *Decline and Fall*, Thomson's *Seasons* and Fielding's *Tom Jones*.

Nearly all the streets approaching Covent Garden have distinguished residents of the literary and theatre world, as well as interesting shops. In King Street, where Samuel Taylor Coleridge lives, writing for the *Morning Post*, are the auctioneers Hutchins & Paterson, who deal mainly in prints and pictures. At Rawthmell's coffee-house in Henrietta Street, the Society of Arts was established in 1754. Bedford Street has been popular for many years, for its excellent mercers, drapers and lacemen, but in the last few years they have tended to move westwards, giving place to second-hand booksellers and more printsellers.

In Maiden Lane Voltaire lodged at a French perruquiers's establishment for several years. In Southampton Street is the firm of Godfrey & Cooke, the oldest established druggist and chemist in London. Long Acre has been the headquarters of the carriage business since the days of Charles I – one of the best firms today is Hatchet's.

At the corner of Long Acre and Bow Street is the shop of Messrs Merryweather, the fire-engine manufacturers, whose business has been here for more than a hundred years. The engraver Charles Grignion has his business in James Street, while in Russell Street there are tradesmen of all kinds among the famous coffee-houses.

In the northern line of shops stretching from Shoreditch to Oxford Street are two old-established firms selling prints and engravings – Colnaghi and Graves. In Cranbourn Alley, which runs from Leicester Square to the north-east, is the shop of Hamlet the silversmith. It has been described as a long, low shop whose windows seem to have no end – and not to have been dusted for centuries, with dim vistas of dish-covers, coffee biggins and centre-pieces. His stock in trade is said to be worth millions, and half the aristocracy are in his debt; seven watchmen stand guard over his treasures every night.

St James's Street we have already reconnoitred for its clubs. Many of its old houses are now let out as lodgings to country gentry, but there are some interesting shops here, particularly on the eastern side. At number 76, where Gibbon died six years ago, is Elmesley's bookshop. At number 29, next door to Boodle's, is Miss Humphrey's shop, selling caricature prints. Number 62 is Laurière's, the jeweller, and on the corner opposite St James's Palace is Sams' library, Mr Sams being both librarian and publisher.

Mr Lock, the hatter, is flourishing and gaining the custom which formerly went to William Finch of Covent Garden. The Duke of Bedford records deserting Mr Finch and buying a fine beaver hat from Mr Lock as long ago as 1759. It cost him £1, and six double cockades were 9 shillings. The Duke of Wellington and the King himself buy their military hats and uniforms at Hawkes, which was established in Piccadilly in 1771, but Nelson buys his uniforms at Gieves, now the country's principal naval tailor, which opened in Portsmouth fifteen years ago.

We have already mentioned Hatchard's, the bookshop in Piccadilly where the Tories meet. Debrett's bookshop nearby is the haunt of the Whigs. In Dover Street, off the north side of Piccadilly, is Joe Manton's gun-shop. It is eight years now since he patented his main improvements in the manufacture of guns, and it has made him the friend of many aristocratic sportsmen. There is yet another publisher in this street, Edward Moxon, who specializes in poetry.

Old Bond Street was built in 1686, and its continuation, New Bond Street, to Oxford Street, was under way by 1721. At first the large, four-storeyed, brick houses were inhabited by people of quality, but very soon it developed into a street of shops, the shopkeepers living over the shops and letting off the extra rooms. The customers are rich, and the shops sell only the best. James Smyth's perfumery shop was one of the first, selling lavender water, wash-balls, pomatum, perfumed powder and soap, and close by Richard Robinson opened his confectionery shop, selling exotic sweetmeats, including comfits, pistachio nuts, prunellos, aniseed and limes, and also flowered jelly glasses.

The number and variety of shops have increased very quickly, catering for all the needs of Mayfair, and today there are book- and music-publishers here, tailors, milliners, perfumiers (including Atkinson's, which was established only last year), jewellers, chemists, druggists, fishmongers, butchers, poulterers, dairymen, tea and coffee merchants, wine and spirit merchants, fruiterers, grocers, cheesemongers, pastrycooks and bakers, porcelain, china and glass shops, woollen and linen drapers, boot- and shoe-makers, tobacconists, gold and silver lacemen, carpet manufacturers, an umbrella- and parasol-maker, furriers, a seedsman and florist, lamp-makers, cabinet-makers and upholsterers, a saddler and harness-maker, a gun-maker, carriage-manufacturers and livery stables.

Ludgate Hill and the streets around Covent Garden were particularly popular for mercers' shops until the better houses began to move westwards, and after 1783, when the Tyburn gallows were removed to the front of Newgate prison, many more shops began to appear in Oxford Street. The pickpockets and footpads disappeared as the building of shops and houses proceeded quickly, and soon even the ghosts whom so many had seen haunting the site of the old gibbet at Tyburn faded away and were forgotten. Only two years later, Sophie v. la Roche was writing to her daughters:

We strolled up and down lovely Oxford Street this evening, for some goods look more attractive by artificial light. Just imagine, dear children, a street taking half an hour to cover from end to end, with double rows of brightly shining lamps, in the middle of which stands an equally long row of beautifully lacquered coaches, and on either side of

George Street, Hanover Square

these there is room for two coaches to pass one another; and on the pavement, inlaid with flagstones, can stand six people deep and allows one to gaze at the splendidly lit shop fronts in comfort. First one passes a watchmaker's, then a silk or fan store, now a silversmith's, a china or glass shop. The spirit booths are particularly tempting, for the English are in any case fond of strong drink. Here crystal flasks of every shape and form are exhibited: each one has a light behind it which makes all the different coloured spirits sparkle. Just as alluring are the confectioners and fruiterers, where, behind the handsome glass windows, pyramids of pineapples, figs, grapes, oranges and all manner of fruits are on show. We inquired the price of a fine pineapple, and did not think it too dear at 6 shillings or 3 florins. Most of all we admired a stall with Argand and other lamps, situated in a corner-house, and forming a really dazzling spectacle; every variety of lamp, crystal, lacquer, and metal ones; silver and brass in every possible shade; large and small lamps. . . .

Up to eleven o'clock at night there are as many people along this street as at Frankfurt during the fair, not to mention the eternal stream of coaches. The arrangement of the shops . . . with their adjoining living rooms, makes a very pleasant sight. For right through the excellently illuminated shop one can see many a charming family scene enacted.

Sophie was obviously fascinated by Oxford Street. A few weeks later she wrote again:

This afternoon I took a walk up that lovely Oxford Street, so as to take a good look at all the houses and the numerous shops. Our imagination, dear children, is not nearly big enough to picture the quantities of inventions and improvements. I found another shop here like the one in Paris, containing every possible make of woman's shoe; there was a woman buying shoes for herself and her small daughter: the latter was searching amongst the doll's shoes in one case for some to fit the doll she had with her. But the linen shops are the loveliest; every kind of white wear, from swaddling-clothes to shrouds, and any species of linen can be had. Night-caps for ladies and children, trimmed with muslin and various kinds of Brussels lace, more exquisitely stitched than I ever saw before. I already wrote you about the petticoats for infants of six months to hoary age. People, I noticed, like to have their children with them and take them out into the air, and they wrap them up well, though their feet are always bare and sockless. . . .

I was glad to strike some of the streets in which the butchers are housed, and interested to find the meat so fine and shops so deliciously clean; all the goods were spread on snow-white cloths, and cloths of similar whiteness were stretched out behind the large hunks of meat hanging up; no blood anywhere, no dirt; the shop walls and doors were all spruce, balance and weights brightly polished. Bread likewise laid out on white cloths; the assistants are decently clad, and the master fairly courteous, though no Englishman will ever pay one compliments for they are not taught cringing respect for people of rank and affluence; they know that their greeting and thanks are unbidden.

Whether they are silks, chintzes or muslins, they hang down in folds behind the fine high windows so that the effect of this or that material, as it would be in the ordinary folds of a woman's dress, can be studied. Amongst the muslins all colours are on view, and so one can judge how the frock would look in company with its fellows. Now large shoe and slipper shops for anything from adults down to dolls can be seen – now fashion articles of silver or brass . . . behind great glass windows absolutely everything one can think of is neatly, attractively displayed, and in such abundance of choice as almost to make one greedy. . . .

Only one or two shops sell women's clothes ready made. When one speaks of 'buying a dress', it means buying a length of material for a dress, which you will either make yourself or have made by a visiting dressmaker. To help with dressmaking several fashion magazines have recently been published. Heideloff's *Gallery of Fashion*, which first appeared six years ago, consists of hand-coloured aquatints of the latest fashions and appears once a month. Another publication, *The Fashions of London and Paris*, claims to contain 'correct drawings of from ten to twenty of the fashionable dresses . . . a work of the highest utility to milliners, dressmakers, and private families in the country and all parts of Europe', while the *Lady's Magazine* and *The Monthly Museum* also give valuable information about the clothes that the *beau monde* is wearing.

There has been a startling change in women's fashion during the last year or two. The fine ladies of London no longer wear the elaborate and ridiculously tall headdresses, stuffed with horsehair, which were so expensive to create that they sometimes had to stay in place for weeks at a time and invariably became verminous. They have lost their monstrously large hats and muslin caps, and the hoops under their skirts. Instead of the silks, satins and brocades of a few years ago, women of fashion have taken to dresses of the flimsiest white muslin. They have dispensed with corsets, reduced underclothes to a negligible shift, raised the waist-line to draw attention to the bosom and lowered the neckline so as almost to expose the breasts.

This new fashion has come from post-Revolutionary France, for

Rowlandson's view of a bonnet shop

among the French immigrants who have fled to London are some of the dressmakers who used to work for the French aristocracy, among them Rose Bertin, Queen Marie Antoinette's dressmaker, who continues to send out her 'fashion dolls', dressed in the latest French fashion, to the Courts of Europe. The fashion began in France after Napoleon Bonaparte's campaign in the eastern Mediterranean – the simple, unornamented dress of the Greek City States was adopted as an ideal dress for the similar culture which the revolutionaries were attempting to establish in France.

Few London ladies have gone to the extremes of the Parisians, but fashionable women now walk abroad in deeply low-cut gowns, the transparency of the muslin revealing a minimum of pink underclothes, and the slit at the side of the skirt showing pink-stockinged legs. Bodices have become so short that waists have virtually disappeared.

With dresses now made of English cotton and muslins, it is the turn of the East India Company to complain of loss of business, but to no avail.

Caps have lost favour and women have taken to a classical-looking bandeau for evening, which is often made of strips of coloured embroidery. Some, still under the eastern influence, have taken to wearing muslin turbans, which for important evening functions they adorn with ostrich feathers, the higher and straighter the better, though no one has yet exceeded the Duchess of Devonshire, who has found one three feet long.

It is this bitterly cold winter, the coldest for many years, that has brought common sense back into London fashion. Already the change is apparent. It is the end of the naked bosom. Stays have come back, and an overdress with puffed sleeves. Long, tight-fitting, lace-trimmed drawers are on sale, for the first time ever. Plaid scarves and cashmere shawls, large fur muffs and woollen spencers are now being worn, and much heavier, warmer cloaks, with ankle boots.

The 'beauty doctors' of London are kept busy these days. Women have been using face powder for years, despite the fact that until recently mercury was used in its preparation, which had a disastrous effect on the skin. Now advertisements claim that preparations are 'entirely without mercury or any such harmful thing in it'. One beauty doctor is advertising night masks, forehead pieces, red pomatum for the lips, a paste to smooth and whiten the hands, a tooth powder to cleanse and whiten the teeth and a plaster to take off hair from any part of the body'. She also '. . . shapes the eyebrows, making them perfectly beautiful

105

without any pain, and raises low foreheads as high as you please'.

Herbalists as well as beauty doctors have now opened shops in London, selling herbal cosmetics and the aromatic waters of lavender, elderflower and rosemary. Scent is used a great deal these days, not only on the person but on linen and clothes stored in presses and chests, and sprinkled about the rooms.

The change in men's clothes has been as great. Today the right thing for a gentleman to wear is a plain tail coat, waistcoat and breeches of fine woollen cloth, and the tall silk hat designed three years ago by a London haberdasher, although when he first appeared in it, there was such a commotion that he was charged with a breach of the peace for having, according to the *St James's Gazette*, '. . . appeared on the public highway wearing upon his head a tall structure having a shining lustre and calculated to frighten timid people. Several women had fainted at the sight, children screamed, dogs yelped and a small boy had his arms broken'.

Another innovator was Thomas Chippendale, who opened his workshop, first in Conduit Court, Long Acre, in 1753, and then at 60 St Martin's Lane. In 1754 he published *The Gentleman and Cabinet Maker's Directory*, which contained furniture designs, some new, some already in use, with directions for making them and with 160 engraved plates. Since his death, in 1779, his son John has continued the business and today has a steadily increasing sale of his beautiful furniture to a large and distinguished clientèle.

It was in King Street, Covent Garden, that West Indian mahogany was first used by cabinet-makers. The story goes that when Dr Gibbons, an eminent physician, was building a house in King Street, his brother, a West Indian captain, gave him some mahogany, which he had brought home as ballast, but the carpenters found it too hard to work, and it was laid aside. Soon after this, when Mrs Gibbons wanted a candle-box, the doctor asked his cabinet-maker in Long Acre to make one of some wood that lay discarded in his garden. Like the builders, the cabinet-maker complained that it was too hard for his work, but the doctor only said he must get some stronger tools. The box was so fine that the doctor had a bureau made of the same wood and, pleased with the colour and polish, invited his friends to come and see it. Among them was the Duchess of Buckingham, through whose patronage mahogany came into general use.

After 1753, mahogany was imported in large quantities, for it is not only heavy and hard but reliable. Many of the houses around Covent Garden, and particularly in King Street, were given mahogany front doors, and then the furniture-makers took to it, using it solid, not as a veneer.

A few years after Chippendale opened his workshop, Hepplewhite established his business in Cripplegate. He too wrote a catalogue, *The Cabinet and Upholsterer's Guide*, but it was not published until 1786, two years after his death, when the business was being carried on by his wife. Hepplewhite furniture is generally rather simpler than Chippendale, though equally attractive, and introduces painting and gilding decoration, as well as inlay of bands of satinwood, rosewood and ebony.

Robert Adam, who died eight years ago, in 1792, was an architect who felt that furniture and decoration should be an integral part of the designs of his buildings. He therefore designed his furniture and passed his drawings on to a practical cabinet-maker, much of it being made in the Chippendale workshops. Many other cabinet makers now copy his designs, and Adam furniture has become a distinctive style – he was responsible for the sideboard as we know it today. Some of his early work was painted with floral sprays on a cream or pale green ground, much of it done by Angelica Kaufmann, who was living in Golden Square during the late 1760s and 1770s; she also decorated the main rooms of some of the London mansions Adam designed, including several of his houses in the Adelphi.

Thomas Sheraton came to London from his home in the north of England ten years ago and has established himself in Wardour Street, Soho, primarily as a designer of furniture. His designs are in some ways similar to those of Hepplewhite but his chairs, in particular, are lighter. His latest piece of furniture, which has only just come onto the market, is the 'chaise longue', an adaptation of the day bed.

The china-maker Josiah Wedgwood and his partner Thomas Bentley opened a decorating shop at Great Newport Street, adjoining their London salerooms, in 1768, but soon found that they needed more room and moved to Chelsea, leasing a plot of land stretching from Upper Cheyne Row to the King's Road. Here they put up sheds, buildings and kilns, and for the next five years Wedgwood biscuitware was brought here from his Staffordshire works, Etruria, by packhorse trains and wagons, for enamelling, painting and glazing. The 150-mile journey took several days, and there was a good deal of breakage on the rough roads, but after the Trent-Mersey canal was cut, the transport of Wedgwood's beautiful ware became much safer.

The Wedgwood painting shops at Chelsea have recently been

Wedgwood and Byerley's showroom in York Street

demolished, but his factory at Etruria and the London sale-rooms are as busy as ever – the business has been continued by Wedgwood's family since his death five years ago.

With the shops so full of their beautiful wares, the streets of London are crowded, and they are also bewilderingly noisy, not only with the clatter of coaches and carts rattling over the cobbles or newly paved sidewalks but with the cries and songs of the scores of itinerant vendors who earn their living by selling their wares or services to passers-by.

The apple-sellers buy their apples in the London markets and sell them in the streets in pennyworths or by the dozen. In winter some have stands at the street corners, set with a pan of lighted charcoal covered with a tin plate on which they roast apples to sell to labourers and hungry boys.

In early June appear the cherry women, selling their Kentish cherries at 6d, 4d or even 3d a pound. These are the cheapest cherries – the better ones can be bought only in the markets and fruiterers' shops. Even so, the street vendors are inclined to give short weight, although some add 'full weight' to their cry.

Some of the women fruit-sellers stand at the doors of the theatres, also selling programmes of the current play. These are printed by the theatre and sold to the fruit-sellers by the hundred. The criers charge a penny a programme, but if the customer also buys some fruit, he gets his programme for nothing.

Green peas are sold in the streets from carts, at 10d, 8d and 6d a peck, and all are quite indiscriminately described as the earliest and most expensive dwarf peas, although these may be selling in the markets at a guinea a quart.

During the summer, hot loaves at one or two a penny are cried from eight or nine in the morning, for breakfast, and from four to six in the afternoon, for the tea table, and in winter their vendors also sell muffins and crumpets, the muffin man ringing his small bell as he walks down the street.

The gingerbread man is also busy in winter, but in summer his basket is full of other cakes, the most popular being Banburys. From May until the end of July, both men and women sell the mackerel which is brought from the west coast every day of the week, including Sundays, before divine service. This is the most plentiful fish in London, and they sell at 1s.6d each at the beginning of the morning, but as the time passes their price reduces very quickly, and it can reach as low as three for a shilling. There is also a short mackerel season in the autumn, but the spring mackerel are most fancied.

Every day of the year milk is carried through the streets in pails suspended on a yoke over the shoulders. It sells for 4d a quart, or 5d for the better kind, although both are usually diluted with water before they leave the milk shops. They also sell cream at 1s.4d a pint. Nearly 7 million gallons of milk are sold each year in London. It is a very profitable trade, and 'milk walks' are sometimes advertised for sale. A milk retailer will sometimes employ two or three carriers, who are nearly always strong, stalwart Welsh girls.

At the end of June and in early July new potatoes are sold wholesale in the markets by the bushel, and the barrows sell them for a penny or 1½d a pound. The rhubarb-sellers are busy, and strawberries are coming in at the same time. They are brought fresh to the markets twice a day, and the street traders sell them in conical baskets containing about a quart, making an average profit of 6d a basket.

A little later in the year comes the lavender, selling at 'six bunches a penny – sweet lavender'.

Cat- and dog-meat sellers are to be found everywhere, and they are always women. They sell horse-flesh and bullocks' livers at 2d a pound, and tripe in penny bundles.

But there are other things sold on the streets besides food, such as bandboxes made of pasteboard or light wood, convenient little articles selling sometimes for as much as 6 shillings, all of them having been made by the crier or his family. You can buy baskets made of rush or osier, to carry your household shopping, and rush or rope doormats, as well as hearth brooms, brushes, sieves, bowls, clothes-horses and clothes-lines, which the vendor may push around in a small cart or carry in a large pack on his shoulders.

The tinker who mends bellows carries his tools buckled in a leather bag to his back and sets up anywhere in the street his work demands. The men who collect brickdust carry it round in small sacks on the backs of donkeys and sell it for knife-cleaning. The chair-menders work in pairs: one carries the bundles of rushes and collects the broken chairs, while the other seats himself anywhere in the street that is convenient and sets to work. Small repairs usually cost a shilling, but a new covering may cost up to half-a-crown, according to the fineness of the rush you want – and this only after a good deal of haggling. The knife-grinder trundles his machine from street to street, grinding and setting scissors for a penny or 2d a pair, pen-knives for a penny each, and table knives for 1s.6d to 2 shillings a dozen.

'Tiddyty tiddyty tiddy-loll Tiddy-doll', the cry of the gingerbread-seller

The sound of a large bell and the cry of 'Dust-O' signals the approach of dust carts. They come through the streets every morning and will empty your dustbin every day, if you like, for no charge, since the two men who accompany each cart are employed by the man who owns it, at a weekly wage. They take the laden carts to the outskirts of the city, where the contents are sifted by women and girls, who separate the cinders and bones from the ash and other refuse. The ashes are sold for manure, the cinder and bones for fuel, and the proprietor makes a fair profit from the business.

'Sand-O' heralds the arrival of the sandman, who sells his sand for cleaning kitchen saucepans and the like – it is also spread over a freshly scrubbed wooden floor to protect it from footmarks. It is sold in packs, red sand costing 2½d a pack and white sand 5 farthings.

Early each morning the Jewish dealers in old clothes call at the servants' entrance of houses to buy the cast-off clothing of their masters which has been passed on to them. The dealers take them to Rosemary Lane, the rag fair adjoining Tower Hill, where they barter or sell them. Here, heaped on the ground, are piles of boots and shoes, hats, umbrellas and old clothes, men's, women's and children's, although some of the better-looking clothes are sometimes draped over chairs or clothes-horses. And amidst all this motley display, the buyers and sellers smoke and shout, doze, bargain and wrangle, drinking tea, coffee and sometimes beer.

There is an exchange for them adjoining Rosemary Lane, but they prefer to trade in the open street.

In bad weather both boys and women sweep the crossings, and beg a reward from those who benefit by their labour. They usually receive a halfpenny and, by choosing the particularly muddy and difficult places, manage to earn enough to make their work worthwhile.

Morocco slippers are sold in the street. There is an old Turk who has sold them in the Strand, Cheapside and Cornhill for many years, and is well known for the soundness of his wares. He sells all sizes and colours, from 1s.6d to 2s.1d a pair. Now he has a few Jewish competitors.

The chimneysweeps patrol the streets soon after dawn, each master sweep followed by two boys, the taller of whom carries the bags of soot and directs the poor little creature who does the actual sweeping. He is usually apprenticed from a parish workhouse and, by being deliberately underfed, is kept small enough to make his way up the narrowest of chimneys. It is a disgraceful business, entailing terrible hardship for the child. Often a boy of twelve or more is so thin and tiny that he looks no more than seven or eight years old.

Jonas Hanway, the benefactor of so many benevolent institutions, who died in 1786, was one of the first to make his complaint effective. He obtained an Act of Parliament which decreed that every apprentice wear a brass plate on his cap, engraved with the name and address of his master, so that if he were unduly ill-treated his master could be reprimanded. But this did not greatly ease the lot of the wretched little sweep. Today, fourteen years later, however, the end of his suffering is approaching. A machine for sweeping chimneys has just been invented and is reported to be thoroughly efficient, so that in future this alone will be used for the necessary but unsavoury task of chimney-sweeping.

Poorest of all the street vendors are the match-sellers, who often sing a low, wailing song and beg as they sell.

St Paul's from the southwest

7. Sight-Seeing – Churches, Public Buildings and Mansions

Today there are 112 churches of the established Church of England in London, and fifty-eight Church of England chapels attached to institutions or private houses. There are nineteen foreign Protestant churches and chapels, including one Armenian, one Danish, six French, eight German and one Swiss. There are twelve Roman Catholic chapels, six synagogues, six Quaker meeting-houses and 133 other meeting-houses and chapels of various sects, including the Methodists, who dissent from the established English Church.

St Paul's Cathedral, the seat of the bishopric of London, stands, as we have seen, in the heart of the City, at the top of Ludgate Hill. It is open for divine service three times a day, at 6 a.m., 9.45 a.m. and 3.15 p.m. At other times it is shut, and to gain admission you should knock at the door in the northern portico and will be allowed in for a small payment.

This is the largest church in the City, Sir Christopher Wren's masterpiece, on the site of a 600-year-old cathedral that was destroyed during the Great Fire. The first stone of the new cathedral was laid in 1675, the choir was ready by 1697, and the last stone was placed in position in 1710, with the dome added in 1711.

With its pillared portico, surmounted by the two towers, St Paul's is built in the Renaissance style but in the form of a Roman cross, giving a longer nave than the Greek cross Wren first planned, and surmounted in the centre by a great dome, the largest and finest church dome in the world, apart from St Peter's in Rome. It is made of wood with an overlay of lead, and inside it is an inner dome of brick; through the centre of these domes is a cone of brickwork which supports the stone lantern and the cross.

There are very few monuments in the cathedral as yet, but on payment of 2d you may inspect the Great Bell and its fourteen-foot pendulum. Admission to the highest gallery, to inspect the outer and inner dome, will cost you 4d and will involve a climb of 534 steps – although the first 260 are easy, the rest are difficult and very dark.

During the years following the Great Fire more than sixty churches were built to replace those which had been lost, and Wren had a hand in many of them, including St Michael's, Cornhill; St Bride's, Fleet Street; St Mary-le-Bow, Cheapside, and St Stephen Walbrook – all with large windows, galleries and simple altars, their tall, stone spires soaring over the rooftops and marking the parishes.

St Michael's, Cornhill, on the east side of St Michael's Alley, was a twelfth-century church of which only the tower survived the fire. In 1672 Wren began the present Renaissance building, with its Doric columns and arches, leaving the tower as it was, but in 1721 it had to be rebuilt. He made it a perpendicular tower, 130 feet high, like the chapel tower at Magdalen College, Oxford.

The earlier St Bride's, Fleet Street, was probably as old as St Michael's. Wren built the present church in 1680, but his spire was struck by lightning in 1754 and is now six feet shorter, being reduced to 226 feet. Until three years ago, the Spital sermons (see p. 80) were preached here, and from early in the century the church has been renowned for its beautiful bells. Two treble bells were added to the ten originally cast for the church, and in 1724 the first peal ever completed in Britain on twelve bells was rung – people still come to Fleet Street especially to hear them.

Even more famous for its beautiful bells is the church of St Mary-le-Bow in Cheapside. This again stands on an ancient site, for the first Bow church was built by the Normans, and it probably acquired its curious name from being the first London church built on stone arches or bows.

The nightly ringing of the Bow bell at nine o'clock was first mentioned in 1315, when the warden had the old bell re-cast. The ceremony was probably a survival of the Norman curfew, when everyone had to be indoors. In 1472 John Dun, a mercer, left money to maintain the ringing of the bell every night at nine o'clock, to direct travellers on their way to London, and in 1520 William Copeland presented a bigger bell, for the purpose of 'sounding a retreat from work'. By the time the church had acquired a full peal of bells, the legend was created that to be a true Cockney you must have been born within their sound.

The old church was completely destroyed in the Great Fire, and Wren began to build the new church, over the Norman crypt, in 1671, completing it in 1683, with a beautiful belltower, more than 200 feet high, and a spire surmounted by a weather vane in the form of a griffin.

St Stephen's, Walbrook, which Wren built between 1672 and

1679, is just behind the Mansion House, replacing a fifteenth-century church. Its tower, spire and exterior are relatively plain, but the interior is exceptionally beautiful. The circular dome, of timber and lead, sixty-three feet high, is carried by eight arches supported by Corinthian columns and is thought to have been an experimental model of the dome of St Paul's.

St Dunstan's-in-the-East, in Tower Street, near the Tower of London, is another church which Wren rebuilt. The spire above the tower stands on four arches, and the interior is Renaissance, with Doric and Corinthian columns and round-headed windows. Today it is sorely in need of restoration, for the roof of the nave is pushing out the walls below.

St Dunstan's-in-the-West is in Fleet Street. The church was built in the eleventh century and miraculously escaped the Great Fire, which stopped three doors away to the east. The old church is in a ruinous condition today, and one feels it cannot stand much longer without some drastic rebuilding, but the great clock is one of the sights of the town, for the hours are struck by two giants, perched on the top of the wall from which it projects. There are a number of flourishing booksellers in the churchyard.

St Andrew Undershaft, in Leadenhall Street, is another celebrated church which escaped the Great Fire. It is said to have received its name from a long shaft or maypole, higher than the church steeple, which early in the morning of May Day used to be set up and hung with flowers opposite the south door of the church until, during the reign of Henry VIII, the ceremony came to an end after 'Evil May Day', when there was rioting after a bitter quarrel broke out between wealthy money-lenders, including the Lombards, and impoverished London artisans and apprentices.

Between 1520 and 1532 the old church was rebuilt, and today it has fine stained glass and a seventeenth-century pulpit and font. Its most important monument is that of the London chronicler Stowe, who died in 1605.

Yet another old City church which escaped the Great Fire is St Giles's, Cripplegate. The original church was founded in the eleventh century and rebuilt after a bad fire in 1545, since when it has been little changed. Oliver Cromwell was married here in 1620, and amongst the famous who have been buried here are John Foxe, the author of the *Book of Martyrs*, Sir Martin Frobisher, the Elizabethan explorer and naval hero, and the poet John Milton – seven years ago Samuel Whitbread erected a bust in the church to his memory.

Moving westwards, St James's, Piccadilly, is another of Wren's churches (see p. 36).

St Martin-in-the-Fields, with its beautiful Corinthian portico, was built between 1721 and 1726, by James Gibbs, a disciple of Wren, on a site in use since the thirteenth century. St Martin's is the parish church of the sovereign, and George I was the first churchwarden of Gibbs' new church.

St Paul's, Covent Garden, was built by Inigo Jones when he was working on the Covent Garden square – a little red-brick church, with a simple Tuscan porch facing the square. Its entrance is on the west side, leading into the small churchyard. Inside the entrance is a wide vestibule, with stairs on the left leading to the organ gallery. To the right is a large vestry, to the left the rector's vestry. The central door in the vestibule leads to the church itself, simple and dignified, with white walls, tall, round-arched windows and an austere altar, behind which are four carved wooden pilasters and a triangular pediment in harmony with the eastern portico. The oak pulpit, with its golden angels, carved by Grinling Gibbons or one of his pupils, stands on the northern side of the main aisle, and the organ gallery is over the western entrance.

Five years ago St Paul's was severely damaged by fire: the roof, painted ceiling and parts of the walls were destroyed. Thomas Hardwick was appointed to rebuild the church and, although there were some who wanted him to make it less austere, he remained faithful to Inigo Jones' original conception.

The congregation is no longer as fashionable as when the church was first built, but many famous names are associated with it. The traveller Lady Mary Wortley Montagu was baptized here, and in the churchyard lie buried Robert Carr, Earl of Somerset, Samuel Butler, Sir Peter Lely, William Wycherley, Pierce Tempest and Grinling Gibbons. Today many of the players from the theatres round Covent Garden are buried here, and people are now calling it 'the actors' church'.

Westminster Abbey is the Collegiate Church of St Peter and the principal church of the diocese of Westminster. It is not the seat of a bishop, so does not have the status of a cathedral, but is under the jurisdiction of a dean and chapter, who are subject neither to the Archbishop of Canterbury nor to the Bishop of London, but only to the sovereign.

With the exception of Edward V, every sovereign since William the Conqueror has been crowned here, and most monarchs from Henry III until the late King George II lie buried here.

In the eleventh century King Edward the Confessor rebuilt the

Horwood's plan of Westminster

ancient little Benedictine abbey on the site, but Henry III rebuilt the Confessor's abbey, and over the years there have been many additions, but it remains an exceptionally beautiful example of Gothic architecture, with its white marble altar and floor of black and white marble flagstones.

Edward the Confessor's chapel is immediately behind the altar, and in the centre is his shrine, with a chest containing his ashes. Here also are the tombs of Henry III, Edward I and Edward III.

The chairs used for the coronation are kept in this chapel. In one of these, enclosed in the seat, is the stone from Scone, which tradition says was Jacob's pillow at Beth-el, on his journey from Beer-Sheba, and which was brought to London by Edward I. Leading from the eastern end of the chapel is the chantry of Henry V, containing his tomb, but the silver head of his effigy, with the sceptre and ball, have long since been stolen.

Round these two chapels there are nine smaller chapels, dedicated to various lesser saints, and at the eastern end of the Abbey is the magnificent chapel of Henry VII, dedicated to the Virgin Mary, which he built as a burying place for himself and his descendants, the first stone being laid in 1502. One of the chapel's most strikingly beautiful features is the fan-vaulted ceiling, the finest and most delicately wrought that England had ever seen.

Today the exterior of the Abbey is in a ruinous state. Sir Christopher Wren began renewing the outer stonework in 1688 but did not have time to complete it. In 1739 Nicholas Hawksmoor built the two west towers, and the roof has recently been repaired again, but the turrets and buttresses are decaying and are in danger of collapse if more restoration work is not undertaken very soon.

From the top of one of the western towers one has a wonderful view of London. There is a charge for ascending the 283 steps, but it is well worth the climb.

Today the abbey is being spoiled by too many monuments, even though some are by Roubilliac and Bacon. In Poets' Corner, for example, which is in the south transept, leading from the Chapel of St Faith, are monuments to Chaucer, Spenser, Shakespeare, Jonson, Milton, Dryden, Thomas, Gay and Goldsmith, as well as Handel and Garrick, giving it the atmosphere of a museum rather than a place of worship.

Southwark Cathedral, near the southern end of London Bridge, is, after Westminster Abbey, one of the finest remaining Gothic buildings in what is now regarded as London, but it is in the diocese of Winchester.

St Margaret's Church, Westminster, is close to the Abbey, one of

The west front of Westminster Abbey from Tothill Street

Westminster Hall: exterior

the two parish churches of Westminster and the parish church of the House of Commons. With many alterations throughout the centuries, it has survived from Plantagenet days and was rebuilt in the Perpendicular style at the beginning of the sixteenth century. Here Samuel Pepys was married in 1655, John Milton the following year.

The beautiful east window was installed only forty years ago, although it had been made some 2½ centuries earlier, when Ferdinand and Isabella of Spain ordered it for the Abbey to celebrate the betrothal of their daughter Catherine to Arthur, Prince of Wales. Arthur died before it was completed, and his younger brother, who became Henry VIII, became Catherine's second husband. The glass was preserved but despatched to Waltham Abbey, for there seemed to be an element of popish superstition in the depiction of the Devil carrying off the impenitent thief, while an angel ministered to the soul of the thief who truly repented. However, over the years, the criticism faded and in 1758 parishioners had the opportunity to buy the window for St Margaret's.

The Speaker and the House of Commons always attend St Margaret's in state on important national anniversaries, such as

Westminster Hall: interior

30 January (King Charles I's martyrdom), 5 November (the Gunpowder Plot), the day of the monarch's accession and 29 May, the anniversary of the Restoration of King Charles II. The sermon is always delivered by the Speaker's chaplain.

Among the many buildings of the Palace of Westminster, Westminster Hall, the House of Lords and the House of Commons are the remains of the old palace built by Edward the Confessor. It stands close to the banks of the Thames, and the stairs leading from the river are still called Palace Stairs.

The House of Lords is the old Court of Requests and was fitted up for the peers only this year, on the occasion of the union of Great Britain and Ireland. This room does not occupy the whole of the court of requests, for part of the northern end has been formed into a lobby, by which the Commons pass to the upper house.

The House of Commons has met here for nearly 400 years. It was originally a chapel built by King Stephen and dedicated to St Stephen. It was, rebuilt by Edward III and made a collegiate church, then surrendered to Henry VI, who gave it to the Commons for their sittings – and they have remained here ever since. Although it has been enlarged, it is far too small for the present number of members, but it is well equipped, and the benches have cushions covered with green morocco leather. There is a gallery along the west end, and the north and south sides are supported by slender iron pillars. The west front of the chapel can still be seen, with its fine Gothic window, but it is sad that the gilded and painted walls of the original building have nearly all disappeared during the alterations.

Beneath the House is an under-chapel, and one small court of the Palace has been left untouched and is now part of the dwelling of the Speaker of the House, whose garden stretches down to the river.

The House of Commons may be viewed at any time, access to the gallery during sittings being by introduction or a written order from a member, or by fee to the door-keeper. No women are admitted during sittings. There is a coffee-room where visitors may dine, and light refreshments can be had in an outer room which is used as a kitchen.

Adjoining Westminster Hall and the Houses of Parliament is a new, plain building containing a number of committee rooms and offices of the House of Commons, but this building has never been completed, and it is shortly to be taken down and an entirely new Parliament House built.

The Tower of London is on the north bank of the Thames, at the eastern extremity of the City, just below London Bridge. Begun by William the Conqueror, it has been greatly extended by succeeding kings and today covers eighteen acres, being used as an arsenal and garrison and also as a state prison. The White Tower is still the central feature, surrounded by an inner ward enclosed by a great wall, in which are built thirteen towers. The outer ward, again protected by a massive wall, has six towers facing the river. Beyond the wall is a wide moat, which most people now regard as a useless nuisance. Spanning the moat is St Thomas's Tower, under which is the sinister Traitors' Gate.

On the river bank, beyond the moat, is a broad wharf, with a platform mounted with sixty-one pieces of cannon, which are fired on State holidays and at times of celebration such as great victories in time of war. At each end of the wharf is a wooden gate, which divides it from the streets and is open only during the day.

Entrance to the Tower from the wharf is by a drawbridge, the principal entrance being to the west, by a stone bridge built over the moat.

Within the walls are several streets and a variety of buildings,

A tour of the Tower menagerie

Fanny Howe, tigress, born in the Tower, 1794

including the church of St Peter ad Vincula, first built in the twelfth century, ordinance offices, the Mint, the record office, the jewel office, the armory, the horse armory, the grand storehouses, houses belonging to the officers of the Tower, barracks for the garrison and two sutling houses, where camp followers sell food to the soldiers of the garrison.

The Tower is governed by an officer of the army bearing the title 'Constable of the Royal Palace and Fortress of London'; at coronations and other state ceremonies he has custody of the Crown and regalia. Under him are a lieutenant, a deputy lieutenant, the Tower major, who is the resident governor, the gentleman porter, the yeomen porter, the gentleman gaoler, four quarter gunners and forty warders. The warders' uniform is the same as that of the yeoman of the guard – a coat with large sleeves and flowing skirts of fine scarlet cloth, with several rows of gold lace round the edges and seams, and a broad, laced girdle round the waist. On the back and breasts are the king's badge (the thistle and rose) in silver and the letters GR. The caps are round and flat.

Prisoners are confined in the warders' houses, but by application to the Privy Council they are usually allowed to walk in the precincts during part of the day, accompanied and guarded by a warder.

In a yard to the right of the western entrance, lions and other wild beasts are kept. There is a bell at the side for the keeper, who for a shilling will show you the animals and tell you their histories. Today you will see lions, tigers, leopards, panthers, the laughing hyena, the Spanish wolf, the ant bear and some mountain cats and racoons.

There were a number of monkeys kept in the yard until a year or two ago, but by the King's orders they have now been removed, for one of the largest attacked a small boy and badly damaged his leg. The keepers take care to protect visitors but warn them not to approach too near the dens and certainly not to play with their occupants.

The animals are well kept in clean and commodious conditions, their dens being about twelve feet high, built in two storeys, with iron gratings in front. They live in the lower part by day and sleep on the upper floor at night.

The animals appear to be healthy, but the keepers say that those who have been whelped in the Tower are more fierce than those taken wild.

In the Jewel Office are the imperial crown, the golden orb, which is placed in the monarch's right hand at his coronation, the golden sceptre, St Edward's staff and the Sword of Mercy which are borne before the monarch in the coronation procession, (the Sword of Mercy between the two swords of justice; spiritual and temporal) and the gold saltcellar of State.

No visitors are allowed to see any part of the Mint, which has been in the Tower since the Norman Conquest.

We cannot leave this corner of London without studying the busy scene of the Port of London which occupies six miles of the Thames, two miles above London Bridge to four miles below. The annual value of the exports and imports of London today is more than £60 million, and the annual amount of customs more than £6 million. This trade employs some 3,500 ships, both British and foreign, and there are usually about 1,100 ships on the river each day as well as more than 3,000 barges and other small craft for lading and unlading, which employ 4,000 labourers. There are 2,288 barges and other craft engaged in inland trade, and 3,000 wherries and similar small boats for passengers, which employ another 8,000 watermen. In addition, there are 1,200 revenue officers and the crews of the vessels.

The Custom House is on the north bank of the river just above the Tower. Built in 1718, it is 189 feet long and has two storeys, the Long Room in the upper storey extending the entire length of the central part of the building. Here the commissioners who manage the business of the customs personally superintend the officers and clerks. On each side of the Long Room and underneath the building are extensive warehouses for housing goods until they are taken away by merchants, and in front of the building are quays with cranes for loading and unloading.

The East India Company is the largest importer to the United Kingdom, and East India House is in Leadenhall Street, close by, where it was built in 1726. Last year it was greatly enlarged to a frontage of 200 feet, which involved the demolition of many small houses, and its impressive portico of six large Ionic columns was built. The full title of the Company is now 'The United Company of Merchants of England Trading to the East Indies' and at present it is responsible for almost one tenth of the country's imports, but there are signs that its monopoly is breaking up. On the renewal of its charter, a few years ago, the Government made important changes, insisting that all despatches be submitted to them before being forwarded to India, for as the Company now trades with 176 million people they want to know precisely what is going on. A Board of Control was established so that the Company's Court of

125

The Custom House

Directors is now subordinate to the Government. Six years ago private merchants were granted leave to export goods in the Company's ships, which meant another curtailment of the Company's power.

Since Pitt's Act of 1784, the new Board of Control has been nominated by the Crown and now consists of an unlimited number of members, all of whom, except two, are members of the Privy Council and include two principal Secretaries of State and the Chancellor of the Exchequer. Only three of the Commissioners are paid, and they are all changed when the ministry changes. They have supreme power to keep or send despatches and have access to all books, accounts, papers and documents in East India House, including orders and secret despatches. So the Company's monopoly is virtually ended and it seems probable that before long private investors will outnumber those of the members of the Company.

Sir John Soane is still working on the Bank of England building, to which he was appointed architect in 1788. The back of the building, looking onto Lothbury, is now completed, with its high stone wall and gateway for carriages into the bullion court, but Soane has not yet finished the main entrance in Threadneedle Street. On the east side of this entrance is a passage leading to the Rotunda, which Soane has modelled on the Pantheon at Rome.

Leading from it are the various offices of the management of each stock.

A recent visitor to the Rotunda described the scene here when the stockbrokers and jobbers arrive:

> Here, from the hours of eleven to three, a crowd of eager money-dealers assemble, and avidity of gain displays itself in a variety of shapes, truly ludicrous to the disinterested observer. The jostling and crowding of the jobbers to catch a bargain frequently exceed, in disorder, the scramble for places of the rudest crowd that assemble at the doors of our theatres; and so loud and clamorous at times are the mingled voices of buyers and sellers that all distinction of sound is lost in a general uproar. On such occasions, which are by no means unfrequent, a temporary silence is procured, by the beadle or porter of the Bank, in the following manner: Dressed in his robe of office, a scarlet gown and gold-laced hat, he mounts a kind of pulpit, holding in one hand a silver-headed staff, and in the other a common watchman's rattle. By an athletic exercise of the latter over the heads of the crowd, he occasions a clattering noise that overpowers the stoutest lungs, and consequently compels the separation of the vociferous mob of stock-jobbers.

When the official Stock Exchange Association was founded in 1773, its members found their own quarters and left the Bank. Those who were not members have stayed on, year after year, but now they have been told to go and to do their business elsewhere, leaving the Bank of England to fulfil its real function in peace.

Its staff consists of a governor, deputy governor, twenty-four directors, chosen annually from among the proprietors, and about 700 clerks. Today it has a balance of £15½ million.

As we have seen, the top shops in the galleries of the Royal Exchange have now been replaced by Lloyd's Coffee-House for underwriters and merchants, the Royal Exchange Assurance Offices, the Merchant Seamen's Offices and the Lord Mayor's Court Offices. The outside shops no longer pay and are disappearing too, but from 8 a.m. until 6 p.m. the Exchange is open as a thoroughfare through which you can walk and study the building which Jerman designed to replace the earlier Exchange, destroyed in the Great Fire.

The Mansion House interior is elegant and spacious, although some of the rooms are rather dark. With a ticket, supplied only by the Lord Major or the sheriffs, you may watch from the gallery the banquet and ball which follow the installation of the new Lord Mayor each year on 9 November.

John Soane, architect

The Guildhall stands at the north end of King Street, Cheapside. It is the seat of the municipal government of the City and its public hall. Here the various courts of the City are held, including the Lord Mayor's Court, where, before the mayor, aldermen and recorder of the King's Bench are heard actions for debt, trespass and similar suits arising within the City and liberties. It is also a Court of Chancery and a Court of Appeal, and the place where suits between master and apprentice are heard. It is regarded as the cheapest in the country, for an action may be begun for 4d and ended for 30 shillings, all within a fortnight.

The British Directory has recently published an account of the numerous courts and offices in the Guildhall:

> The Court of Common Council consists of the Lord Mayor, aldermen and representatives of the several wards, who assemble in Guildhall as often as the Lord Mayor, by his summons, thinks proper to convene them. They annually select from among themselves a committee of twelve aldermen and twenty-four commoners, for letting the City lands, to which end they generally meet at Guildhall on Wednesdays, whereof two aldermen and four commoners are a quorum. They appoint another committee of four aldermen and eight commoners for transacting the affairs belonging to the benefactions of Sir Thomas Gresham, who generally meet at Mercers' Hall by appointment of the Lord Mayor. They also, by virtue of a royal grant, yearly appoint a governor, deputy and assistants, for managing the Irish estates. They have likewise a right of disposing of the offices of town-clerk, common serjeant, judges of the Sheriffs' Court, common crier, coroner, bailiff of the borough of Southwark, and City garbler.

Here also are the Court of Common Hall, the Sheriffs' Courts, the Court of Hustings (place of elective assemblies), the Court of Wardmote, the Court of Conservancy (board controlling a river or port), the Court of Requests or Court of Conscience (to settle all disputes between citizens where the debt is under 40 shillings), the Court of Escheator (escheat is the reversion of property to the Crown if the owner dies, intestate and without heirs), the Chamberlain's Court, the Court of Orphans (the Lord Mayor and aldermen being guardians to the offspring of all freemen who die before their children are twenty-one), the Court of Hallmote, Pie-Powder Court (dealing with any troubles that may arise from St Bartholomew's Fair) and the Justice Hall Court in the Old Bailey, held eight times a year for the trial of offenders within the City of London and the county of Middlesex, the judges being the Lord Mayor, the aldermen, the recorder and the sheriffs, as well as at least one of the nation's judges.

Sir Christopher Wren repaired the fifteenth century Guildhall after severe damage in the Great Fire, but it is now in dire need of restoration.

The Excise Office is in Old Broad Street, built in 1768, on the site of Gresham College, which was demolished to make way for it. Twenty-nine articles are included in the Excise laws, including ale,

'On 'change'. Figures by Rowlandson, architecture by Nash

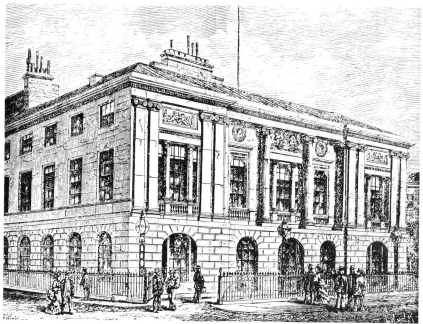

Trinity House

beer, cider, wine, malt, soap, glass and paper, producing an annual revenue of £10½ million.

Trinity House is well worth a visit. It is a new building in Trinity Square, just above the Tower of London on Tower Hill, designed by Samuel Wyatt and completed only five years ago, to replace the old Trinity House which stood in Water Lane, Lower Thames Street, a little to the north-west of the Customs House.

The corporation was established in 1515 by Henry VIII, to superintend the interests of shipping, both military and commercial, and all naval matters not under the express jurisdiction of the Admiralty. In 1680 they built their first lighthouse, all previous lighthouses on the English coast having been built by private individuals, under a patent from the Crown. They bind and enrol apprentices to the sea; examine the mathematics pupils from Christ's Hospital; examine mathematical masters for the Navy; and place and alter when necessary all the buoys, beacons and sea-marks along the English coast. They also survey the channel of the Thames and other ports; give licences to poor, aged and maimed mariners to row on the Thames without licence from the Watermen's Company; hear and determine complaints from officers and men in the merchant service, and have the power to punish seamen for mutiny or desertion. The Corporation consists of a master, deputy master, thirty-one elder brethren and an unlimited number of younger brothers, for any seafaring man may be admitted into the Society, though without the power of any control in its concerns. The elder brethren are usually selected from commanders in the Navy and merchant service.

The interior of Trinity House, in particular the hall and court room, is very elegant, with many interesting portraits. With a recommendation from the resident secretary, strangers may view it by giving the servant a shilling.

Visitors also like to see the forty-nine halls of the City Companies, used for the management of the affairs of the companies and also for feasts on public holidays and occasions of special celebration. Among the most impressive halls are the Ironmongers' in Fenchurch Street, the Merchant Taylors' in Threadneedle Street, the Goldsmiths' in Foster Lane, the Grocers' in Grocers' Alley, Cheapside, the Stationers' in Stationers' Court, Ludgate Hill, the Drapers' in Throgmorton Street, and the Apothecaries' in Blackfriars.

Many of the Companies are extremely rich, amongst the most wealthy being the Mercers, Grocers, Drapers, Fishmongers, Goldsmiths, Skinners, Merchant-taylors, Haberdashers and Ironmongers; they distribute large sums each year to charities, and several have established excellent schools.

Law students usually spend two or three years at one of London's Inns of Court after coming down from Oxford or Cambridge. The most important of these inns is at the Temple, the stretch of land on which it stands running north to south from Fleet Street to the river and east and west from Lombard Street to Essex Street, off the Strand. It once belonged to the Knights Templars and then to the Knights Hospitallers of St John of Jerusalem, who granted the land to the students of the common law of England. It is now divided into two societies, the Inner and Middle Temples, each consisting of the bencher, barristers, students and members. In term-time the students dine in the hall of their society, thereby 'keeping commons'. To dine a fortnight in each term is 'keeping the term', and twelve of these terms qualifies a student to be called to the bar, which means he is entitled to plead and manage cases for clients in court. The Benchers examine the students and call students to the bar or reject them, without appeal. This in itself is a cause for dissatisfaction, for students are sometimes rejected on political grounds, and there is a feeling that they should be under a higher jurisdiction.

The fees are not high. A student at the Inner Temple pays £4.2s.

Part of the Inner Temple

to the Society, plus a duty to the King of £16.4s., while terms are kept for about 10 shillings a week, and a student can dine there very cheaply.

The Inner Temple has a lovely riverside garden; the Middle Temple garden is smaller, and not so well placed, but the hall is spacious and elegant, and the beautiful Temple Church belongs to both societies.

The other principal Inn of Court is Lincoln's Inn, on the west side of Chancery Lane. Its constitution is similar to that of the two societies of the Temple, but the terms of admission and the time taken to qualify are slightly different.

There are several smaller Inns of Court in London, including Gray's Inn, on the north side of Holborn, named after the Lord Gray who once had a house there; Staples Inn, in Holborn; Thavies Inn, which is an appendage to Lincoln's Inn, situated near St Andrew's Church in Holborn; Serjeant's Inn in Chancery Lane; Lyon's Inn in Wych Street; Clifford's Inn, near St Dunstan's in Fleet Street, an appendage of the Inner Temple, and Clement's Inn near St Clement's Church in the Strand.

Back in the west end of London, in Piccadilly, Burlington House has become an important meeting-place for Whig politicians.

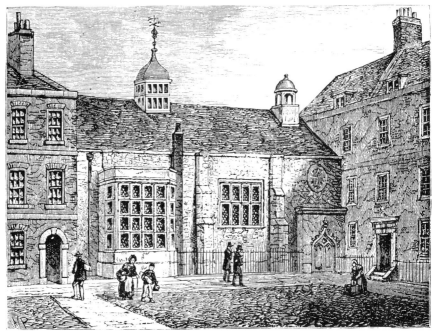

Staples Inn

In 1718 the third Earl of Burlington encased the front of the original red-brick house with stone, and the height of many of the first floor rooms was raised, in order to convert them into impressive rooms of state. Colin Campbell built the colonnade, and the street wall with its large gate was rebuilt.

Horace Walpole, the poet and essayist who died three years ago, was entranced by the colonnade. 'Soon after my return from Italy, I was invited to a ball at Burlington House,' he wrote. 'At daybreak, looking out of the window to see the sun rise, I was surprised with the vision of the colonnade that fronted me. It seemed one of those edifices in fairy tales that are raised by genii in a night-time.'

Yet the comfort of the splendid Palladian mansion has been sacrificed to the magnificence of the reception rooms, and the rooms on the ground floor are, by comparison, rather small and cramped. This provoked some criticism from the late Lord Chesterfield:

> Possess'd of one great hall for state
> Without a room to sleep or eat;
> How well you build let flattery tell,
> And all the world how ill you dwell.

Nevertheless, a recent owner, the late Earl of Portland, entertained lavishly and was a kindly patron to men of letters as well as musicians and theatre people. The German composer Handel lived here for three years, and the writers Pope and Swift were frequent visitors. Today the Cavendishes of Portland maintain the tradition of generous hospitality.

Devonshire House, the home of the Dukes of Devonshire, to the west of Somerset House and facing the Green Park, was built by the third Duke about sixty years ago, replacing an earlier mansion destroyed by fire. It is set back from the road, so that the garden side looks onto the south side of Berkeley Square. Kent was the architect, and the exterior is plain and austere, surrounded by its high brick wall, as are all the great London mansions, as a protection against midnight prowlers and the occasional rebellious mob. The architect Decimus Burton has added the semi-circular bay on the garden side, with a magnificent staircase of marble and alabaster, with handrails of solid crystal.

The present (fifth) Duke and his beautiful wife Georgiana, daughter of the first Earl Spencer, have made Devonshire House a Whig stronghold – it is the Duchess, not her rather lazy husband, who is the driving force of the powerful Whig circle which meets here so often, including the Prince of Wales, Charles James Fox and the dramatist Sheridan. The Duchess is in her forties now but her beauty, charm and championship of the cause of the Whigs are unimpaired.

Lady Reade's elegant white house in Curzon Street, opposite the Mayfair Chapel, stands back from the roadway, amid well-tended lawns and plane trees. It was built during the reign of Queen Anne, at a time when there was hardly any building of importance between its garden and Piccadilly, and Lady Reade has now commissioned Sir John Soane to make extensive alterations.

Chesterfield House stands where South Audley Street and Curzon Street now meet, but when it was built it faced along the desolate Tyburn Lane to Hyde Park, of which it had an uninterrupted view, and its garden stretched back along the north side of Curzon Street to the garden of what is now Lady Reade's house.

Chesterfield House, built by Isaac Ware and completed in 1752, is composed of a central block joined by two colonnades to two large wings. The central part has two floors and an attic storey above a basement, which is protected by iron railings, and the entrance is reached by three shallow steps. The five long sash windows on the first floor are pedimented, and each has a wrought-iron balcony.

The Deaf Judge or *a Mutual Misunderstanding*

'The staircase particularly will form such a scene, as is not in England,' wrote Lord Chesterfield a couple of years before the house was finished. 'The expense will ruin me, but the enjoyment will please me.' The staircase *is* truly magnificent, a double stairway of white marble, each step made from a single block twenty feet long. The two branches sweep upwards from the main approach to meet the triple-arched landing, and the baluster is of the most delicate ironwork. The staircase and the columns of the screen facing the courtyard were bought at the sale of the Duke of Chandos's possessions at Canons, when that house was demolished in 1744. A copper-gilt lantern made to hold eighteen candles came from a sale of Sir Robert Walpole's Houghton Hall, and furniture and hangings have been collected from all over Europe.

Serjeants' Inn

Devonshire House

There are six reception rooms on the ground floor. French looking-glasses hang on the pale blue walls of the boudoir, and the chairs are covered with petit-point embroidery of flowers on a white background. The Italian drawing-room has an outstandingly beautiful marble mantelpiece, and in the white-and-gold drawing-room, with its crimson-flowered silk hangings, are exquisite French furniture and china cabinets filled with Sèvres and Chelsea porcelain. The picture collection includes works of Titian, Rubens, van Dyck, Poussin, Canaletto, Guido, Salvator Rosa and Tenier.

The most interesting and entertaining people of Mayfair society used to appear at Lord Chesterfield's parties, but as he grew older and increasingly deaf, he withdrew more and more from society, content in the seclusion of his library and garden, while Lady Chesterfield lived apart, devoted to good works and to the evangelism of John Whitefield. Lord Chesterfield died in 1773, and Chesterfield House has now passed to his cousin, the fifth Earl, who maintains it in all its splendour.

81 and 82 Pall Mall were originally one house, built during the Commonwealth and (like Nell Gwynne's old house, 79) had a garden at the back with a terrace giving a view of the royal gardens. It is named Schomberg House, after a Dutch general who came

Nell Gwynne's old house on Pall Mall

over with William III and was killed at the Battle of the Boyne. After that it had a succession of tenants, and it was Astley, the artist, who divided it into three separate dwellings. After his death, the artist Cosway occupied the central portion, and the portrait-painter Gainsborough lived in the west wing until his death twelve years ago. Since then it has become a gallery for the exhibition of pictures and other works of art.

At the western end of Pall Mall, almost completely surrounded by its high brick wall, is Marlborough House. It was built by Wren for John, Duke of Marlborough, for his London residence, and after his death his Duchess Sarah continued to live here, in a style of great grandeur, until her death in 1744. The house then stood empty for some years but was eventually bought by the Crown, and members of the royal family have lived there ever since.

Carlton House, on the north side of the Mall, is the residence of George, Prince of Wales. The mansion was built for Lord Carlton in 1709 and bequeathed to his nephew, the Earl of Burlington, from whom Frederick, Prince of Wales (father of King George III), bought it in 1732. The Prince made many additions and improvements to the simple, red-brick mansion, and the result is a palace of princely magnificence, with a Corinthian portico and a fascinating, gently winding double staircase, the two flights meeting on the first floor, dividing again and curving upwards to meet on the floor above.

His Majesty was not born at Carlton House but (in 1738) at old Norfolk House in St James's Square, on loan to Prince Frederick after he had left St James's Palace as a result of his quarrel with his father, George II. When, shortly afterwards, Prince Frederick moved to Leicester House, the Duke of Norfolk returned to Norfolk House, a very old mansion with a large courtyard in front, and began the building of the present Norfolk House, although the ruins of the old house can still be seen at the back of the handsome new building.

Within the last fifty years many more mansions have been built in London – for example, Lansdowne House, Cambridge House, Gloucester House and Apsley House, while Mrs Montagu, 'Queen of the Blue Stockings', moved to her new mansion in Portman Square (Montague House) about twenty years ago. She had watched its building with delight: 'It is an excellent house, finely situated, and just such as I have always wished but never hoped to have', she wrote to a friend, and Horace Walpole described it as '. . . a noble, simple edifice. Magnificent, yet no gilding. It is grand, not tawdry, not larded, embroidered, and ponponned with shreds and remnants, and *clinquant* like the harlequinades of Adam, which never let the eye repose an instant.'

8. Entertainment

London offers entertainment in both summer and winter. For music-lovers there are concerts of the Academy of Music, at the Crown and Anchor tavern in the Strand, and concerts of Ancient Music are held in the Hanover Square rooms. There are theatres and opera houses, exhibitions of pictures and other works of art, and amusements of all kinds at the Pantheon in Oxford Street, at Astley's and in the gardens of Vauxhall and Ranelagh.

The Academy of Music opened many years ago, in 1710, when a group of composers and performers arranged to study and play together, meeting at the Crown and Anchor tavern – the first subscription was half a guinea. Their performances were helped by the gentlemen of the Chapel Royal and St Paul's Cathedral, and amongst their keenest attendants was the composer Handel, who had just arrived from Germany.

In 1732, after some misunderstanding between the Academy and Mr Gates, Master of the Chapel Boys, the boys were withdrawn. The Academy then undertook to train and educate four boys at its own expense, and the number of members was increased and the annual fee raised to 1½ guineas. In 1747 ladies were admitted and, soon after, the Academy meetings became public concerts, and eminent singers and instrumentalists were engaged. In 1785 the original laws and rules of the Society were reconsidered and confirmed, and members decided to move to the Freemason's Hall in Great Queen Street. The orchestra was improved and augmented, and Dr Arnold was appointed conductor.

All went well for the next few years, and the Academy was increasingly respected. In 1792 the subscription was raised to 5 guineas and the orchestra was again improved. Last year the Academy returned to the Crown and Anchor tavern, where Dr Arnold has continued to conduct with distinction. There are usually eight concerts during the season, beginning in January and continuing at fortnightly intervals. Occasionally members introduce modern composers, which gives variety to the concerts, but mainly they keep to the old masters whom all know and love.

141

Rehearsal for a revival of Thomas Arne's oratorio Judith, *first performed in 1761*

The Society which produces the Concerts of Ancient Music comprises members of the original Academy of Music who broke away some years ago. Their recitals are held in a concert room on the eastern side of Hanover Square, beginning in February and continuing weekly each Wednesday until the end of May. Six directors, chosen from the nobility, take it in turns to choose the programmes, but they are always of ancient music. No modern composers are ever chosen and it is a strict rule that no composition less than twenty-five years old may be selected, under pain of a considerable fine for the director. This has happened only twice during the society's history, but it is, of course, a discouraging state of affairs for any young composer anxious to hear his work performed, and it makes for a lack of variety in the concerts.

Opera is performed mainly at the Theatre Royal, in Bow Street, Covent Garden where much of Handel's work was first heard, but there is also a theatre on the west side of the Haymarket (burned down a few years ago, in 1789, but at once rebuilt) which concen-

142

Interior of Covent Garden theatre

trates entirely on opera. Its scenery is rich and brilliant, but there is not so much space behind the curtain as in the old theatre. The opera season begins in December, and the presentations are every Tuesday and Saturday until June.

In 1720 a company of French actors at a then new theatre in the Haymarket, opened with a temporary licence from the Lord Chamberlain. Some ten years later an English company were performing there, and it came to be called 'The Little Theatre in the Haymarket', but when, in 1766, it received its full patent, it became 'The Theatre Royal in the Haymarket'. Today it is still flourishing, in the hands of the Colman family, although greatly in need of restoration and modernization. It is open for the presentation of plays and English opera from 15 May to 15 September, and various new works are produced there in the course of each season.

Those who prefer drama to opera should also seek out the Theatre Royal in Drury Lane, where Sarah Siddons and her brother John Kemble are the stars, under the management of Sheridan. No better acting can be found anywhere in the country than at this splendid new theatre (successor to one which opened in 1663), but, brilliant as Sheridan is in so many ways, he is no financier, and behind the scenes trouble is brewing, for he is heavily in debt and many of the players are owed considerable arrears of salary.

The art of acting has developed considerably since the young David Garrick arrived at Drury Lane in 1742. Within five years he was jointly managing the theatre and was to rule there until 1776. His acting was different from anything that had been seen before: '. . . when little Garrick bounced on the stage it seemed as if a whole century had been swept away and a new order at once brought forward, bright and luminous, and clearly destined to dispel the barbarism and bigotry of a tasteless age, too long attached to the prejudices of custom and superstitiously devoted to the illusion of imposing declamation,' wrote one critic.

For all his artistry, Garrick did not yet adapt realism in stage costume, declaring that audiences would never accept it. He played Lear in breeches, white shirt and ermine-trimmed coat, Macbeth in a Court suit, embroidered with gold. But he served the theatre well. He brought order to the stage and cleared away the stage boxes, so that the actors had it to themselves. He made many practical improvements, particularly in regard to lighting, and appointed Dr Arne as musical director. He insisted on regular, punctual rehearsals and inspired his players with his own spirit of naturalism, so that Drury Lane has become a theatre where people come to enjoy the acting as much as to see the play. Garrick introduced the first Drury Lane pantomime and at last began the dress reforms which were to develop into stage realism.

Garrick retired just over twenty years ago, when Sheridan took over from him, and a year or two later Sarah Siddons appeared at Drury Lane to much acclaim. It was her second appearance – her first had been a failure, but she had gained experience in the provinces and learned her craft well, probably by studying Garrick. Since then she has proved herself one of the most compelling tragediennes the theatre has ever known. All fashionable London comes to see her. Like Garrick, she is an individualist – for example, despite Sheridan's protest, she has insisted on deviating from Mrs Pritchard's long-established interpretation of Lady Macbeth in the sleep-walking scene. After the first time she played it her way, James Sheridan Knowles, who was playing opposite her, declared that, as she set down the candle and wrung her hands in anguish, 'I smelt blood! I swear I smelt blood!'

Dorothy Jordan, the Irish comedy actress, has made history at Drury Lane, where she arrived from Dublin fifteen years ago. She plays not only leading women's parts, in which she is regarded as second only to Kitty Clive, but also sometimes takes male or 'breeches' parts. In 1790 she became the mistress of the Duke of Clarence, by whom she has already had several children.

Sarah Siddons as Lady Macbeth

Drury Lane was doing well, but it was all too clear that the theatre was becoming very dilapidated. It was condemned as unsafe, and Sheridan had to set about raising the money for a new building. The theatre was pulled down almost entirely, although Wren's foundations were left. The company was moved to the Theatre Royal in the Haymarket until Drury Lane re-opened six years ago, with another lavish production of *Macbeth*, in which both Sarah Siddons and her brother John Kemble starred and received the acclamation they deserved. Today that brilliant company is as popular as it ever was, despite what the near future may hold, because of Sheridan's continuing financial troubles.

Sadler's Wells, at the southern end of Islington, in north London, is a popular resort today, both for its entertainment and for the medicinal properties of its waters.

In 1683, Mr Sadler, a surveyor of the highways, decided to develop the spot as a pleasure garden. He found an old music room and began to rebuild it, and during the work one of his workmen discovered a well, which in the Middle Ages had been renowned for its waters' healing powers – the music room had been built for the entertainment of health-seekers. Soon the surrounding fields were daily filled with carriages bringing the nervous, the hypochondriac, and the asthma and indigestion sufferer to drink the waters, for which they were charged a guinea for a season or 6d a glass, with lively entertainment in the music room.

On the death of Sadler, Frances Forcer became the proprietor and his son gave exhibitions of rope-dancing and tumbling. By 1765 Mr Rosoman had taken over, and he replaced the wooden music room with a brick building which soon became a theatre, with a regular company of actors. Today it is as lively and enjoyable a place as it ever was, the plays being varied with ballad operas, musical interludes, pantomimes and acrobatic feats such as tight-rope walking, ladder dancing and tumbling, egg-dancers and performing dogs.

A 3 shilling ticket for a box entitles you to a pint of port, and a second pint will cost you a shilling.

The Pantheon is a large place of entertainment on the south side of Oxford Street, and since the Stuart playwright Vanbrugh's opera house in the Haymarket (successively known as the Queen's Theatre, the King's Theatre and Her Majesty's Theatre) was burnt down in 1789, it has been equipped as an opera house. Eight years ago it was again destroyed by fire, but it was rebuilt and remains today another popular resort of opera-lovers.

The Pantheon

In 1771 the Pantheon also began to offer dancing and other entertainments, and from the outset it was a success – over 2,000 people attended the first ball, among them several peers. The Pantheon then set out to rival Mrs Cornelys' pleasure house close by, in Soho Square. Mrs Cornelys was a German by birth and began her career as a singer. She came to London in 1756 and bought Lord Carlisle's mansion on the east side of Soho Square, where she gave masquerades, balls and concerts to her annual subscribers. But soon there were rumours of scandalous affairs taking place in Carlisle House, and when the Pantheon opened, so near at hand, it drew away more and more of her customers. In 1773 the *London Magazine* wrote: 'The play-houses, the operas, the masquerades, the Pantheon, Vauxhall, Ranelagh, Mrs Cornelys, the London Tavern etc are all crowded. . . . The money squan-

Carriages waiting outside the Haymarket theatre

dered at the last masquerade was computed to be £20,000, though tradesmen go unpaid, and the industrious poor are starving.'

Horace Walpole had watched the Pantheon being built, and a year before it was ready for the opening celebration wrote to his friend Sir Horace Mann: 'The pillars are of artificial *giallo antico*. The ceilings even of the passages are of the most beautiful stuccos in the best taste of grotesque. The ceiling of the ball-rooms and the panels are painted like Raphael's *loggias* in the Vatican: a dome like the Pantheon glazed. It is to cost fifty thousand pounds.'

Extravagant as she was, Mrs Cornelys could not compete, and she was declared bankrupt. She obtained possession of the house again for a short time but was soon in even worse difficulties and was imprisoned in the Fleet. She escaped during the Gordon Riots when the prison was destroyed, and found refuge in Knightsbridge, where she survived by selling asses' milk, deserted and forgotten by all her old patrons. Then she was arrested again; her house was put up to public auction and she was taken back to the Fleet prison, where she died in 1797.

Astley's Amphitheatre, in the Westminster Road, near the southern end of Westminster Bridge, is the place to go for remarkable displays of horsemanship. Philip Astley set up his riding school there a few years after his discharge from the army in 1766, with the announcement: 'Activity on horseback of Mr Astley, Serjeant-Major in His Majesty's Royal Regiment of Light Dragoons. Nearly twenty different attitudes will be performed on one, two and three horses, every evening during the summer at his riding school. Doors to be open at four, and he will mount at five. Seats, one shilling; standing places, sixpence.'

Astley was only twenty-four and had no money, so the riding school at this juncture was only an enclosed piece of ground in the fields between Blackfriars and Westminster Bridge, but he was successful. He was also fortunate, for he had been teaching without a licence. One day when King George III was riding over Westminster Bridge on a particularly restive horse, which became almost unmanageable, Astley happened to see him and showed his ability to subdue the horse so promptly and efficiently that the King gave him his licence, overlooking the lapse.

The riding school was uncovered at first, but Astley was soon able to build a stand with a few covered seats, so that he could advertise his performance 'every evening, wet or dry'.

Horace Walpole wrote to Lord Strafford in 1783: 'I could find nothing at all to do, and so went to Astley's, which indeed was much beyond my expectation. I did not wonder any longer that Darius was chosen king by the instructions he gave to his horse, nor that Caligula made his horse consul. Astley can make his dance minuets and hornpipes.'

Astley now began to collect wood in order to build a fully covered arena for his displays, buying up the scaffolding that had been erected at the funeral of the King's mother, Princess Augusta, and the hustings which had gone up during the last election. With this he was able to build his new riding school, with a stage, two tiers of boxes, a pit and a gallery – he called it 'The Royal Grove'. By this time his son was working with him, proving himself as skilled a horseman as his father, and with other expert riders they were devising dramatic spectacles, the first called *The Death of Captain Cook*

In 1793, when war broke out with France, Astley accompanied the Duke of York to the Continent, superintending the embarkation of cavalry, but the following year he was recalled to London, with the news that the Royal Grove and nineteen adjoining houses had been destroyed by fire. He at once set to work to rebuild the Grove, making it larger and more elegant, and today it stands as the Amphitheatre of Arts, with music and theatrical entertainments, and still with superb displays of horsemanship.

Vauxhall Gardens

One of the most fashionable places to visit during the summer months is Vauxhall Gardens, near Lambeth Palace. There you will meet the cream of London society, including, on occasion, the Prince of Wales himself.

The early history of Vauxhall House and its garden is obscure, but Sir Samuel Morland leased it in 1675, and a contemporary, John Aubrey, wrote that Sir Samuel had built a fine room '. . . the inside all of looking-glass, and fountain very pleasant to behold; which is much visited by strangers. It stands in the middle of the garden, covered with Cornish slate, on the point whereof he placed a punchinello, very well carved, which held a dial, but the winds have demolished it.'

The next account, by Sir John Hawkins, says that the house had been rebuilt since Sir Samuel Morland's time, with a great number of stately trees, and laid out in shady walks. It obtained the name 'Spring Gardens' and, the house being converted into a tavern, it was frequented by 'votaries of pleasure'.

In 1732 the house and gardens came into the possession of Jonathan Tyers, who advertised it as a *ridotto al fresco* – an open-air pleasure-ground – and as more and more people came to visit it, he developed his garden into a place of entertainment for summer evenings. He decorated the garden with paintings, engaged an orchestra, with an organ, and issued silver tickets of admission for the opening night at one guinea each, admission after this being at first 1 shilling and later 2 shillings.

The gardens cover eleven acres and, as one visitor has described them: 'The principal part of the gardens resolves itself into a kind of long quadrangle, formed by four colonnades which inclose an open space, with trees, called the Grove.'

On the visitor's right, standing at the entrance '. . . extends one of the colonnades, some three hundred feet long, with an arched, Gothic roof, where the groins are marked by lines of lamps, shedding a yellow-golden light, and the pendants by single crimson lamps of a larger size at intersections . . . at some distance the entire vista beyond appears one rich blaze of radiance'. He describes another part of the quadrant, lit in a different way, by a '. . . chandelier of great size, formed by coloured lamps, and by various smaller chandeliers'.

Looking across the interior of the quadrangle – the Grove – midway is seen the lofty orchestra, glittering all over with the many-coloured lights diffused from innumerable lamps. . . . Beneath the vast shell which forms the roof of the sounding board of the orchestra many of our greatest vocalists and performers have poured forth their strains to the delight of the crowded auditory in front. . . . The Grove is illuminated not only from the reflected light from the colonnades on either side and by the orchestra, but by festoons of lamps, gracefully undulating along the sides of the colonnades from one end to the other.'

The principal supper room is the Hall of Mirrors but there are supper boxes inside each of the long colonnades. The rotunda is a handsome building with boxes, pit and gallery and a stage for ballet performances; the pit can also be used for displays of horsemanship. Two years ago the first firework display added an even greater excitement to the evening's entertainment.

In the more distant and darker parts of the garden are trees and foliage, rockeries and fountains, with statues and enticing shady walks for lovers.

Addison, Hogarth, Goldsmith, Garrick and Dr Johnson were among the men of letters who loved to visit Vauxhall in past years. After a visit in 1760, Oliver Goldsmith wrote: 'The satisfaction which I received the first night I went there was greater than my expectations; I went in company of several friends of both sexes, whose virtues I regard and judgements I esteem. The music, the entertainments, but particularly the singing, diffused that good humour among us which constitutes the true happiness of society.'

Jonathan Tyers died in 1767, and there have been one or two managers since then, but the gardens still belong to the Tyers

A Gala night at Vauxhall Gardens

family, and the standard of entertainments has been admirably maintained. Today the admission is a shilling, but more on nights of special illuminations. The gardens are open from the middle of May till the end of August. The doors open at 7 p.m. and the concert begins at 8 p.m. The average attendance is 5,000 but on special occasions 15,000 people may be present.

Tyers' idea for Vauxhall Gardens must have come from the creation of Marylebone Gardens which, though much smaller, had been designed on similar lines, with music and scenic entertainment, and which were highly fashionable and successful for many years. The gardens were on the east side of Marylebone Lane and at first entrance was free, but then, in order to keep the company select, a shilling entrance fee was charged, on the understanding that the visitor was to receive the equivalent of one shilling's worth of refreshments.

Handel's music was often played here, under the direction of Dr Arne, and in 1753 the gardens were extended by the inclusion of an adjacent bowling-green. Breakfasts were now served, as well as dinners, and it was also opened every Sunday evening, when 'genteel company' were admitted free to walk, and were accommodated with light refreshments.

Yet the gardens began to decline in popularity after this, mainly because of the highwaymen who were infesting the streets approaching Marylebone and who sometimes came into the gardens. Dick Turpin strolled in one day, approached a highly respectable Mrs Fountayne, who was taking the air, boldly kissed her and, before she could recover from her surprise, bade her 'Good Morning' and strolled away without being detained.

Several attempts were made to maintain the gardens prosperously, but in 1778 they were closed. Six years ago they were opened again for a short time, but with no more success, and now the site is covered with the houses of Upper Wimpole Street.

Ranelagh House and its garden adjoined the Royal Hospital in Chelsea, and when, in 1733, they were put up for auction, they were bought with a view to creating an even more elegant pleasure garden than Vauxhall. The authorities of the Royal Hospital opposed the scheme but were unable to prevent it, and saw with consternation the huge rotunda being built close by. The gardens were opened in 1742 with a public breakfast and a blaze of publicity.

Most of the first visitors were enthusiastic, marvelling at the rotunda and its tiers of boxes, its large floor for dancing and concerts, and its magnificent chandeliers, as well as the Temple of Pan and the Venetian Temple, both of which had been added to the gardens. Others were doubtful, especially in the first weeks: 'The pomp and splendour of a Roman amphitheatre are devoted to no better use than a twelve-penny entertainment of cold ham and chicken,' declared one visitor. A Frenchman writing in the *Gentleman's Magazine* in 1742 said that, 'dumb with surprise and astonishment', he found himself

> . . . in the middle of a vast amphitheatre, for structure Roman, for decorations of paint and gilding, as gay as the Asiatic; four grand portals in the manner of the ancient triumphal arches, and four times twelve boxes in a double row, with suitable pilasters between, for the whole interior of this wonderful fabric – save that in the middle a magnificent orchestra rises to the roof, from which depend several large branches, which contain a great number of candles enclosed in crystal glasses, at once to light and adorn this spacious rotunda. Groups of well-dressed persons were disposed in the boxes, numbers covered the area, all manner of refreshments were within call, and music of all kinds echoes, though not intelligibly, from every one of these elegant retreats.

The Rotunda, Ranelagh Gardens, 1750

But the Frenchman quickly became weary of the glitter and noise: 'In five minutes I was familiar with the whole and every part; in the five next indifference took place; in five more my eyes grew dazzled, my head became giddy, and all night I dreamed of Vanity Fair.'

Horace Walpole was by no means impressed with his first visit: 'I was there last night,' he said, 'but did not find the joy of it. Vauxhall is a little better for the garden is pleasanter, and one goes by water.' Two years later he changed his opinion: 'Every night constantly I go to Ranelagh, which has totally beat Vauxhall,' he wrote. And by 1748 he was saying: 'Ranelagh is so crowded that in going there t'other night in a string of coaches, we had a stop of six and thirty minutes.'

At first morning concerts were given in the rotunda, but when employers complained that young men and apprentices were being lured from their work, the hour of opening was changed to the early evening, the management providing a succession of masqued balls, firework displays, puppet shows and concerts, at which some of Handel's oratorios were performed, while food and drink were served in the privacy of the boxes.

One of the most memorable occasions was the Grand Masqued Ball of 1748, held to celebrate the Peace of Aix-la-Chapelle, when George II attended and there were said to be 2,000 visitors. 'It was by far the best understood and prettiest spectacle I ever saw – nothing in a fairy tale ever surpassed it,' wrote Walpole, and he went on to describe the marquees in the garden, the maypole round which masqued peasants danced to the music of pipe and tabor, the huntsmen with their horns, the harlequins and scaramouches in the little temple on the mount, the gondola on the canal, the orchestras hidden away in secluded corners of the garden, the little shops outside the rotunda, selling Dresden and Japanese china, the booths for tea and wine, the gaming tables and the dancing, and the orange trees, with a small lamp glittering in each orange.

The ball was so successful that another masquerade was held a few weeks later. The King again attended, and also the Duke of Cumberland. All the ladies of the Court were there '. . . in vast beauty, Miss Pitt with a red veil which made her look gloriously handsome . . . Miss Chudleigh was "Iphigenia" and so lightly clad

Embarking for the river crossing to Vauxhall. The young man exclaims,
'O be carefull [sic] my love – don't expose your leg.'

155

that you would have taken her for Andromeda. The maids of honour were so offended that they would not speak to her.'

Handel's *Messiah* and Dibdin's *Ephesian Matron* were heard at Ranelagh in those days, and in 1764 Mozart, at the age of eight, was brought to London by his father to give a performance there on harpsichord and organ.

Throughout the 1760s and 1770s Ranelagh remained fashionable and saw many glittering occasions – as in the summer of 1776, at Lord North's regatta, when the whole river from London Bridge to the Ship tavern at Millbank was covered with pleasure vessels and on both sides of the river bad liquor with short measure was plentifully retailed. Yet the commentator who wrote, 'In a word, from the mixed multitude of lords and liverymen, pinks and pickpockets, dukes and dustmen, drabs and duchesses, the whole scene afforded an admirable picture of High Life below Stairs and Low Life above', indicates that the glory was beginning to dim. Ranelagh was no longer exclusive but was visited by rich and poor alike.

Within the last twenty years, although the gardens are open on Mondays, Wednesdays and Fridays, and there are still special celebrations for royal births and marriages, as well as grand subscription parties, Ranelagh's popularity is steadily fading and attendance on ordinary occasions falling. Society is no longer amused and the proprietors are having to make obvious economies. The standards of entertainment and catering are lower, and with it the moral tone, which was never particularly high. Respectable ladies still walk in the gardens during the daytime, when admission is only a shilling, but few would care to be seen there in the evening, except for a special gala night, graced by some celebrity such as the Duchess of Devonshire, when tickets cost anything from up to 2 guineas. Ordinary evening tickets are only half a crown; a 5 shilling ticket includes a supper of beef, ham, savoy cake, veal, pastry, jelly and blancmange, with wine extra.

For many, Ranelagh has become tedious, involving little more than an endless promenade round the rotunda, while after dark the journey from London is more hazardous than ever, because of the increasing number of footpads. Today it has become so sadly run down that there seems little chance of its ever recovering its former status, and people are beginning to talk of its being closed down.

In 1759, more than twenty years before the Royal Academy began to display its pictures at Somerset House, the British Museum was opened at Montagu House in Bloomsbury. One would like to describe it as another of London's entertainments, for there is much there to see and enjoy, but until there is a change in terms of admittance and an improvement in facilities to examine the exhibits, a visit cannot be truly described as enjoyable.

The Government acquired Montagu House after the death of the second Duke of Montagu, for they were looking for suitable accommodation for Sir Hans Sloane's natural history collection, his library of more than 50,000 books and his valuable collection of manuscripts of Robert Harley, Earl of Oxford, as well as the library of Sir John Cotton, all of which had been left to the nation. Fifty trustees were appointed to run the museum, make the rules and choose the librarians and other officers.

There are three departments – books, natural history and manuscripts, but admission is very restricted, the rules laying down that an applicant has to write for a ticket, stating his name, address and profession and the exact time he wishes to pay his visit. If the officer considers the applicant suitable, he gives the porter permission to give him a ticket when he next applies for it, but not more than ten tickets may be issued for any particular time, and the visitor is allowed only a short visit to each department, each of which has a different officer in charge. In the rules, an hour in each department is allowed, but in practice one is usually hustled round in only a few minutes.

This cumbersome system has not changed since William Hutton, the historian of Birmingham, described his first visit there sixteen years ago.

> We assembled on the spot, about ten in number, all strangers to me, perhaps to each other. We began to move pretty fast, when I asked with some surprise, whether there were none to inform us what the curiosities were as we went on? A tall, genteel young man in person, who seemed to be our conductor, replied with some warmth, 'What! would you have me tell you everything in the Museum? How is it possible? Besides, are not the names written upon many of them?' I was too much humbled by this reply to utter another word. The company seemed influenced; they made haste, and were silent. No voice was heard but in whispers. . . . It grieved me to think how much I lost for want of a little information. In about thirty minutes we finished our silent journey through this princely mansion, which would well have taken thirty days. I went out much about as wise as I went in. . . .

When Sophie v. la Roche visited the museum two years later, she described the 'magnificent edifice' in her usual enraptured style and mentioned the Magna Carta, Roman and Etrurian antiquities and some interesting relics of Captain Cook, but said that, 'There is hardly time to take note of everything one would like to see.'

There are still complaints that there is too much restriction in the library, for although anyone can make use of it for study and reference, after proper application through the principal librarian, the transcription from manuscripts is strictly limited to one or more brief extracts. However, the management is now being altered and conditions are gradually becoming easier. The number of books in the library is increasing as well as the exhibits, which now include relics from Ancient Egypt, displayed in a separate Department of Antiquities.

The Royal Society is the oldest scientific society in the country, having been established by Charles II, although the nucleus of this Royal Society for Improving Natural Knowledge had been meeting since 1645, at Gresham College. These men of science maintained a regular contact with Continental philosophers and scientists, so that they were all able to keep abreast of the scientific experiments and discoveries of the times. At their early meetings one of the most important functions was, wherever possible, to perform and demonstrate these experiments, and the results were published from time to time in their *Philosophical Transactions*.

In 1710 they were established in Crane Court, off Fleet Street, with Sir Isaac Newton as president. Twenty years ago, under the presidency of Sir Joseph Banks, the society moved to its present quarters in Somerset House.

From the time of the society's inception, the Government has appealed to it for advice in connexion with scientific undertakings of national importance. They include the improvement and equipment of the Royal Observatory at Greenwich, in 1710, when it was placed in the sole charge of the society; the change of the calendar, in 1752; the ventilation of prisons; the protection of ships and buildings from lightning; expeditions to observe the transits of Venus in the Pacific, in 1761 and 1769, under the command of Captain James Cook, and the Antarctic expeditions of 1772, also under Captain Cook, who journeyed on to circumnavigate the globe.

The Society of Antiquaries also has rooms in Somerset House, which contain its library and the beginnings of a museum, which includes some recently acquired Egyptian antiquities. Meetings are from November till the end of the Trinity term, on Thursday evenings at 7.30. The subscription is 2 guineas a year, but dis-

Greenwich hospital from the river

tinguished foreigners are given an honorary admission and members are allowed to introduce visitors.

The Society for the Encouragement of Arts, Manufacture and Commerce, in John Street, Adelphi, gives rewards for useful inventions and discoveries, and from money coming from voluntary subscriptions and legacies has already placed nearly £50,000 for improvements in agriculture, chemistry, dyeing, mineralogy, the polite arts, manufacture and mechanics, in addition to suggestions for improving conditions in the British colonies and the settlements in the East Indies.

Meetings are every Wednesday at 7 p.m., from 4 October to 1 June, and membership is by proposal and ballot. Ladies are admitted to membership – among them, until her death this year at the age of eighty, Mrs Elizabeth Montague, and strangers may attend meetings, by applying to a member for an order.

The society, which was established in 1753 and is supported entirely from voluntary subscriptions, has a valuable library, and models, or drawings of models, are on exhibition from 10 a.m. to 2 p.m. every day, except Sundays and Wednesdays.

The Royal Institution in Albemarle Street was founded only last year, 'for the Purpose of diffusing the Knowledge, and facilitating the general introduction, of useful mechanical Inventions and Improvements; and for teaching, by Courses of Philosophical Lectures and Experiments, the Application of Science to the common Purposes of Life'.

This institute is already considered one of the most useful undertakings ever established in London. There is a library, equipped with a number of scarce and valuable historical, classical and scientific works, and a room for reading the newspapers. On the first floor is Professor Davy's mineralogical collection and a semi-circular lecture room, with rising, cushioned benches for 900 people, and accommodation for 200 more in the gallery.

In the basement are kitchen stoves, roasters and boilers, according to the plans of Count Rumford, as well as apparatus for heating water by steam. Professor Humphry Davy reads chemistry lectures three days a week, and there are plans for lectures on mechanics, physics, natural philosophy and astronomy, botany and ancient and modern architecture. The funds come from the proprietors and subscribers, the 400 proprietors each paying 100 guineas and the life subscribers 30 guineas on election.

Londoners love exhibitions. Only last March a new one opened just off Old Bond Street, with the announcement:

'The real embalmed head of the powerful and renowned usurper, Oliver Cromwell, with the original dies for the medals struck in honour of his victory at Dunbar, are now exhibited at No. 5, in Mead Court, Old Bond Street (where the rattlesnake was exhibited last year); a genuine narrative relating to the acquisition, concealment, and preservation of these articles to be had at the place of exhibition.'

A street trader has devised a moveable pantomime, which gives a great deal of amusement. He has a series of coloured prints in a box, which the spectator views through a magnifying glass, while the showman tells the story. The perpetual climbing of squirrels in a wire cage above the box rings a row of bells on top of the cage, which is the signal for the showman to pull the string which changes the print in the box to the appropriate scene. The charge for this entertainment is a halfpenny or penny. There are also many displays of performing animals, and O'Brien, the Irish Giant, who is nearly nine feet high, exhibits himself at 61 Haymarket.

A sport favoured by rich and poor alike is cock-fighting, and there are at least two cockpits in Whitehall, and many others throughout the City. Bear-baiting and bull-baiting are no less

Hyde Park on Sunday

popular. There is no horse-racing in London, but the Derby was
first run at nearby Epsom, in Surrey, twenty years ago.

Everyone plays cards, and most people bet. At home, where
people play whist or quadrille to while away a long winter's
evening, they sometimes make small bets of a few pence, to make
the game more interesting, and this is harmless enough, but in the
clubs of Pall Mall and St James's, where the play is usually faro or
hazard, the betting is sometimes reckless and can lead to terrible
losses, ending sometimes in tragedy.

The annual State lottery is another field for gambling – people
often buy tickets from agents at unscrupulously inflated prices.
Apart from gambling, many seem to bet on the smallest incidents
of daily life.

The most colourful free entertainments in London are regattas
on the Thames. Describing the first one, held a few years ago, the
writer says:

> Every barge, boat, wherry, and lighter was on the river, crowded with
> people. Flags were flying; guns were fired; bands were playing; the
> houses from which the regatta could be witnessed were filled with
> people; the bells of St Martin's were rung in the morning; those of St

161

Margaret's in the afternoon. The chief point of attraction was West-minster Bridge, which was crowded with people, while the avenues at both ends were covered with gaming-tables. The boats on the river were supplied with drink in great abundance, but very bad and in short measure. Every passage to the waterside was guarded by men who took toll, from a penny to half a crown. Scaffolds were erected on the banks, where seats sold for large sums. In a word, the town had gone off its head for a new thing.

Before 1783, when the gallows were removed from Tyburn to Newgate prison, public executions were regarded by some as an entertainment and galleries were erected round the gibbet, with seats which were let at high prices.

Duelling did not begin in England until the sixteenth century and cases were rare. There were more during the following two centuries and the subject is mentioned in the *Tatler* and the *Spectator*. Only four years ago, in 1796, William Pitt and George Tierny fought a duel. As yet no one has been brought to trial for these fights, but public feeling against duelling is growing very strong, for at least half of them involve a fatality.

9. Medicine, Surgery and Hospitals

Today forty-one children out of every hundred die before the age of five, but fifty years ago the rate was seventy-five per cent. The mortality rate of adults, and particularly women in childbirth, has also decreased appreciably, and people are living longer, considerably more than half surviving into their seventies, and about ten per cent into their eighties.

This is evidence of the greatly increased knowledge that doctors and surgeons have acquired of the functions of the human body, particularly during the last twenty or thirty years. They have learnt by observation and research, yet their progress has been slow, partly because of an inherent conservatism which has made people cling to old 'cures' (despite the fact that they do not cure) and partly because progress has depended, in many ways, on the advancement of pure science. For example, doctors cannot yet take an accurate pulse, for watches have only minute hands, nor can they take a temperature accurately, for there are no clinical thermometers yet, while the only sedative to ease agony during surgery is a liberal dose of alcohol, and the death rate under the surgeon's knife is still lamentably high, estimated today at two out of every three operations.

But we now have an accurate knowledge of the physiology of the human body in relation to its anatomy, thanks to the greatest surgeon of our times, John Hunter, who died only seven years ago. The human anatomy had been described by Vesalius in 1543, when he published his book *On the Fabric of the Human Body*, but in order to determine the relation of the structure to the workings of the living body, Hunter carried out experiments on animals which had died in the menageries at the Tower of London.

Established in a house in Golden Square, he began to practise as a surgeon and in 1768 became a surgeon at St George's hospital and began to take pupils at his home. In his later years, at a house in Earl's Court, he continued his research on living creatures, including fish, lizards, blackbirds and hedgehogs, which one of his former pupils, Edward Jenner, sent him from time to time.

The Royal College of Physicians

During the past twenty-five years a large number of hospitals have been established in London, mainly by humanitarians, to accommodate the sick and indigent. As this has meant the assembly of a number of sick patients under one roof, it has greatly helped the advance of medical knowledge through observation.

The Royal College of Physicians, founded by Henry VIII in 1518, was a powerful body by the beginning of this past century, but only men who had studied at Oxford, Cambridge or Trinity College, Dublin, were admitted to full membership. These Fellows were a small but august body who charged high fees and received handsome incomes from their treatment of the rich. Licentiates of the College were members who had studied at Edinburgh or one of the European medical schools, of which Leyden then had the highest prestige. They had flourishing practices, mainly in London or the large provincial cities. Not only were there too few of these

164

doctors, but their charges were too high for most people, who sought advice mainly from apothecaries, originally mere dispensers of drugs from doctors' prescriptions but later advising on their own account.

No one can legally practise in London today as a physician or surgeon without a licence or diploma from the Royal College of Physicians or the Royal College of Surgeons. However, anyone can sell medicine to the public without being a member of the Society of Apothecaries, and despite the frequent attempts of the College of Physicians to prevent mercenary impostors and ignorant pretenders posing as doctors, the sale of quack medicine is today on the increase.

London is now visited by medical students of anatomy, surgery and medicine from all over the world, and eight to 900 come here each year for lectures at the hospitals. Moreover, though private practitioners are gradually gaining sound knowledge, it has been estimated that the patient in a hospital still has a tenfold greater chance of recovery than one receiving private treatment.

Among the principal hospitals in London today, St Bartholomew's, in West Smithfield, is the oldest, having been established during the reign of Henry I. It was here, in 1619, that Harvey first lectured to his students on his great discovery of the circulation of blood.

In 1730 the old hospital was entirely rebuilt, the cost being met by public subscription.

Today the surgeon and lecturer to the medical students is Dr Abernethy, who makes little distinction between a rich man and a poor one – in fact, he is said to be rather more attentive to the poor man.

Accident cases are admitted to the hospital at any time of the day or night, and the sick gain free admission for treatment on application to one of the governors, who meet every week to consider petitions, although at one time you had to put down a burial fee of 19s.6d at the time of admission, which was returned if you recovered. There are always a number of out-patients, and the hospital is attended by the most eminent physicians and surgeons in the City. It is an excellent school for students of medicine and surgery, who visit the hospital in the course of their training.

St Thomas's Hospital, Southwark, is another old foundation, having been established by Edward VI. Its new building was opened in 1732. Today it has twenty wards, each under the care of a Sister and two or three nurses, and there are 485 beds.

The Tower Hill Esculapius. Doctor Van Cheatall displays his charlatan wares

Guy's Hospital, Southwark, stands on the south side of St Thomas's Street and was established in 1725 by the philanthropist Thomas Guy, a bookseller of Lombard Street, who made a fortune by printing and selling Bibles, and probably also by a fortunate investment in South Sea stock. It has accommodation for 400 patients, including rooms for people who have become hopelessly insane. Obstetric physicians have recently been added to the staff, as well as surgeons and professors not engaged in the care of the patients but who lecture and demonstrate to medical students.

The London Hospital, Whitechapel, founded in 1740, began as a dispensary and today is considered one of the most useful charities in the City. The building was completed in 1752, with thirty-five wards and 439 beds. It has a fixed income of about £13,000 a year, derived from legacies, voluntary donations and various funded properties, and is open to any sick person or casualty of an accident.

St George's Hospital, Hyde Park Corner, was opened in 1733, having been converted from Lanesborough House into an infirmary by a group of governors who had seceded from Westminster Hospital. It depends mainly on voluntary contributions, not being richly endowed. Its present income from subscriptions is little more than £2,000, but contributions are generous enough for continuous improvements and extensions to be made to the original building, and since the hospital opened it has treated more than

150,000 patients, a large proportion of them from the poor living within a mile of the hospital.

Westminster General Infirmary in James Street, Westminster, was established in 1719 for the relief of the sick and needy. It was London's first subscription hospital, founded by the endeavours of Henry Hoare who, with a small group of associates, made an appeal to promote the charity. The hospital first opened in Petty France, when it was announced that, 'For the satisfaction of the subscribers and benefactors, and for animating others to promote and encourage this pious and Christian work, this is to acquaint them that in pursuance of the foresaid charitable proposal, there is an infirmary set up in Petty France, Westminster, where the poor sick who are admitted into it are attended by physicians, surgeons, apothecaries, and nurses, supplied with food and physick, and daily visited by some one or other of the clergy; at which place the society meets every Wednesday evening for managing and carrying on this charity, admitting and discharging patients etc.'

Accident cases are freely admitted, without question, at any time of the day or night.

Close by, and connected with the hospital, is the Westminster Training School and Home for Nurses, established to train women

Guy's Hospital

The Middlesex Hospital

for work in hospitals and with private families. The School has undertaken to provide the hospital's entire nursing staff.

The Middlesex Hospital was first established in 1745 in Windmill Street, Tottenham Court Road, for sick and lame people and as a lying-in hospital for married women. In 1755 it moved to its present site in Mortimer Street, and since then additional wings have been built. Nine years ago special accommodation was provided for cancer patients, and two years later the hospital became a refuge for many French Royalists driven from France by the Jacobin Reign of Terror.

Recently the governors have decided that the midwifery patients, numbering about a thousand a year, should no longer be treated at the hospital but attended in their own homes by medical officers from the hospital.

The British Lying-in Hospital in Brownlow Street, Long Acre, was established in 1749, the Lying-in Hospital for Poor Married Women in Aldersgate in 1750, and the City of London Lying-in Hospital, Old Street, City Road, also for poor married women, in 1751. The Westminster Lying-in Hospital in the Surrey Road, near the southern end of Westminster Bridge, was opened in 1756, for poor pregnant women, whether married or not, as were the Queen's Lying-in Hospital at Bayswater Hall in the Oxford Road

The smallpox hospital at King's Cross

and the Lying-in Hospital in Store Street, Tottenham Court Road, all three opening in the 1760s.

Two charities for delivering pregnant women in their own homes were established in 1757, one of which employs thirty-two midwives, and a new Lying-in Charity for the wives of the Foot-guards is being organized at the present time, its headquarters to be at 5 Great Ryder Street.

In 1746, in the fields between Hyde Park and Chelsea, the Reverend Thomas Scott established the Lock Hospital for sufferers from venereal disease, and in Paddington another was built on the site of an old leper hospital – the term 'Lock' being probably derived from the Saxon word 'log' or 'loc', meaning shut or closed, and referring to the isolated state in which lepers are kept. Several more Lock hospitals have recently been established, including the converted Leper Hospital in Kingsland, East London, and the Hospital Misericorda in Goodman's Fields. All the sites chosen are as far as possible from the crowded City.

Although there are so many new hospitals nowadays, the treatment of patients and the administering of preventive medicine is still very much a matter of trial and error, and no great advance on the treatment that was given during the Great Plague of 1665.

Amongst many the theory still persists that to maintain a state of health the four humours, blood and choler, both associated with heat and energy, and phlegm and melancholy, associated with cold and moisture, should exist in the body in the correct proportions. This is why, they argue, blood-letting should take place in feverish conditions, so that the excess of humour which is destroying the balance will depart.

When a physician recommends blood-letting he will be present, but the operation is done by a surgeon – those who cannot afford a surgeon will go to an apothecary. The incision is usually made in the neck or arm. First a handkerchief is thrown over the patient's head, so that he will not see the blood. The doctor then places a ball of wool in the patient's hand, and as he presses it, the vein of the arm swells. The surgeon touches a blue vein with his lancet, and as the blood spurts out the doctor catches it in a basin. He orders the blood-letting to stop when he considers the right amount has been taken, which in the case of a fever is eight ounces. This treatment has been used for years, but more and more people are beginning to realize how futile it is.

It was Sir John Pringle, the army physician, who observed that gaol fever or typhus was the same as hospital fever. Until fifty years ago, many regarded this disease as an unavoidable scourge, but Sir John noticed that it occurred where people were in contact with decomposing matter. He ensured that in the hospitals under his charge the drainage was adequate and the water supply as pure as possible. He even suggested the use of substances which he called antiseptics.

The need for pure water and better water supplies is now realized, but in London they are a long time coming, and in the meantime citizens suffer still from terrible cholera epidemics, despite the fact that deep wells and springs are now used in preference to surface water, streets are cleaned and some are being widened and paved. Ancient open drains are being covered and the pestilential Fleet ditch is at last filled in.

Surgeons are extending the field of their operations but are constantly disappointed, for although in the initial stages the operations appear to be successful, the ultimate death rate is still about two in three – mainly, it is felt, because they are not following the advice of Sir John Pringle and taking proper antiseptic precautions. Operating theatres have no running water, and the floors are sprinkled with sawdust to cover the blood. The surgeon wears an old, blood-stained coat kept specially for the work. Instruments receive only a perfunctory cleaning, and probes, scissors and sponges pass from one patient to the next and from wound to wound. Midwives, too, go from case to case without sterilizing their instruments, thereby spreading puerperal fever and death among their patients.

The last victim of the Great Plague died in 1669, and after that time it did not reappear either in London or anywhere else in the country – no one yet knows why. But now a new scourge has appeared, smallpox, which is taking as many lives – early in this past century it was killing a tenth of the population every year. In 1717, Lady Mary Wortley Montagu, wife of the Ambassador to Constantinople, reported home that the Turks fought the smallpox by 'engrafting' or 'inoculation', and she outlined the method to doctors on her return home. An inoculation hospital was eventually established in London and had a certain measure of success, but it was found that sometimes people who had been treated in this way infected those who had not been inoculated at all.

Over the past quarter of a century, Edward Jenner has solved the problem. He observed that not only did people become immune to the disease after a mild dose of smallpox but that cowmen, after handling cattle suffering from cowpox, do not develop it at all. Two years ago he published his *Inquiry into the Cause and Effects of the Variolae Vaccine*, and his method, which he called vaccination, was accepted, but it received a serious setback when one enthusiast, George Pearson, began applying the virus from cows near London which had been accidentally contaminated and produced not a mild form of the disease but severe eruptions. Notwithstanding, Pearson planned to establish an institution in London for free vaccination, using his defective vaccine but only last year it was discovered what was wrong with it, and his scheme was abandoned. Thereupon the Royal Jennerian Society for the Inoculation of the Cow Pox was instituted. Now several houses are being established in London where people can, without any recommendation, be inoculated free, the principal house, from which the organization is directed, being 14 Salisbury Square, Fleet Street.

The Bethlem (Bedlam) Hospital for Lunatics is on the south side of Moorfields, built in 1675 at a cost of £1,700, which was raised by public subscription.

It was originally intended to accommodate 150 lunatics, but it is now far too small, with more than 250 patients crowded behind its grim walls. A recent visitor, passing from the noisy babel of the seedy second-hand furniture shops and booths which fill Moorfields these days, spoke of the 'strange sense of utter deser-

The Cow Pock — or — the Wonderful Effects of t

noculation! — Vide the Publications of ỹ Anti Vaccine Society.

Mr Jenner's new invention. A satire by Gillray

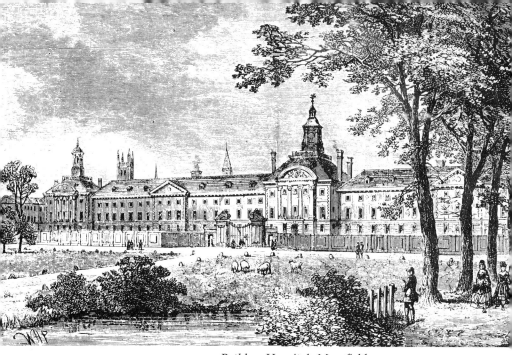

Bethlem Hospital, Moorfields

tion' that came over him as he approached the hospital, and of seeing the 'long gloomy line of cells, strongly barred, and obscured with the accumulated dust, silent as the grave, unless fancy brought sounds of woe to your ears'.

The building is divided into two wide galleries, one over the other, running the whole length of the building, but each divided into two parts with iron gates, women one side, men the other. Patients are admitted on petition to the governors and committee, who sit at the hospital every Saturday.

Conditions at Moorfields, though at first reasonably good, have rapidly deteriorated. Now, at last, the House of Commons has appointed a committee to investigate its conduct and management. They have reported some terrible conditions. They found

> . . . about ten patients, each chained by one arm or leg to the wall, the chain allowing them merely to stand up by the bench or form fixed to the wall, or to sit down. For dress, each had only a sort of blanket-gown, made like a dressing gown, but with nothing to fasten it round the body. The feet were without shoes or stockings. Some of these patients were lost in imbecility – dirty and offensive. Associated with them were others capable of coherent conversation, sensible and accomplished. Many women were locked up in their cells, chained, without clothing and with only one blanket for a covering. In the men's

174

wing, six patients in a side room were chained close to the wall, five were handcuffed, and one was locked to the wall by the right arm as well as by the right leg. Except for the blanket gown, these men had no clothing; the room had the appearance of a dog-kennel. Chains were universally substituted for the strait-waistcoat. Those who were not cleanly, and all who were disinclined to get up, were allowed to lie in bed – in what state can be imagined.

In one cell they found a patient named Norris, who, being a powerful man, had attacked his keeper after he considered he had been improperly treated. As a punishment he was fastened by a long chain which passed through a hole in the wall to an adjacent cell, where the keeper remained in safety and was able to drag the prisoner close to the wall whenever he felt inclined. When Norris tried to prevent this, by wrapping straw round the chain, the gaoler devised a different method of keeping him quiet. An iron ring was riveted round his neck, from which a short chain, ending in a ring, was made to slide up and down on an upright bar, more than six feet high, which was riveted into the wall. Another iron bar, about two inches wide, was fixed round his body, and on each side were projections encircling both his arms, so that they were pinioned to his sides. This meant that he could raise himself to stand against the wall but could not step away from it and could not lie down, except flat on his back. This was how he was condemned to live for the next twelve years, and during all that time it was reported that his conversation was perfectly rational.

Until thirty years ago, Bethlem was considered one of the sights of the town, and anyone who had a fancy to see people in such dire distress could visit the hospital, by paying a fee to one of the attendants. This money was estimated to add £400 a year to the hospital's income.

In 1751 St Luke's Hospital was established on the north side of Moorfields. Also a lunatic asylum, it was independent of Bethlem, being a charity organized by a group of benefactors who felt that Bethlem had become quite inadequate for indigent lunatics.

St Luke's provided a place of refuge and medical aid for outcast maniacs, and at the same time a school was established here for the study of insanity. The first physician in charge was Dr Battie, who allowed other doctors to study his method of treating his patients. One important fact which emerged was that the custom of allowing visitors to Bethlem, for no better purpose than to gape and snigger at their wretched condition, was doing a great injury to the patients, and due to the influence of St Luke's the treatment at

Norris chained

Bethlem has improved. Now the number of visitors is strictly controlled. They are admitted, only with a governor's ticket, on Mondays, Wednesdays and Fridays, while friends of the patients may visit every Monday and Wednesday, from ten to twelve in the morning.

When Sophie v. la Roche paid a visit to the asylum a few years ago, although she was probably not shown some of the worst conditions, she found things better than she had expected and showing the influence that the treatment of patients at St Luke's was already having:

> We came to a broad passage, thoroughly well lit, with cells on either side, just as in a monastery. An attendant opened some cells, and I noticed the inspector showed a kindly tact as he explained, 'You will see here a man who has been very ill,' or 'here is someone who is very ill.' The cruel expression 'fool' or 'madman' never once passed his lips. . . . The inspector and attendant spoke gently and kindly to them all, especially to the invalids who are kept locked up, since otherwise they might inflict wounds upon themselves and others . . . these unhappy folk had no chains or straps to rub sores if they made frenzied gestures with their arms and hands and so aggravate mental stress by further pain. They wore a strong jacket with long white sleeves, tied behind their backs; this forms a sufficient deterrent to their harming anything with their hands and does not hurt them in any way; if they should show signs of restlessness while strolling around loose, they are fastened to the corner of the room with strong cords, also fixed to the jacket. They can move backwards and forwards in a semicircle, so preserve a certain amount of freedom, yet are rendered harmless without having to suffer.

The inspector told Sophie that, '. . . it was Dr Monro's institute, and he had forbidden them to ill-treat or frighten any one of the unfortunates either by word or threat or mien'. 'This is a fever of the mind,' continued the inspector, quoting Dr Monro. 'Tender, gentle handling is the only cure for this. Where the fever has proved infectious to the body, I shall try to relieve it by diet and medicines.' And the inspector added, 'Such persistent tenderness and kindness must inevitably have a salutary effect, for the worst attacks improve within a fortnight or three weeks, and a number are cured.'

In the women's side, Sophie saw many young girls, some of them very beautiful, whose reason had been impaired by abortive marriage plans. The inspector told her that this was the chief

177

Rowlandson's sketch of the women's ward at St Luke's Hospital for the Insane

reason for their madness: 'Young ones mourn a lover's faithlessness, his death, or the parents' harshness at not agreeing to the marriage, mainly because they had already made marriage contracts for their daughters which they had no intention of changing, regardless of the fact that the poor girl may have positively disliked the husband planned for her and was deeply in love with someone else.' Another cause of madness, said the Inspector, was found among the older women from the Methodist Church '. . . usually from childbed, when they are in any case very frail and the strict doctrines of this sect made them anxious, which gradually gives way to a quiet kind of lunacy; but these cases were mostly cured'.

Last year a site of nearly twelve acres for a new asylum was bought in St George's Fields, Lambeth, and plans are now being made for Bethlem to be moved there.

There are also more than 300 private homes for lunatics in London, for insanity is said to be on the increase. There is no Government control at all of these private establishments, and there have been some scandalous affairs recently of unwanted wives or other relatives being taken to one without realizing at first what was happening to them, and then being locked away and not heard of again, unless they manage to escape or somehow make contact with a friend to help in their release.

The Magdalen Hospital in St George's Fields is for girls and young women who have become wretched outcasts from society through having been seduced under promise of marriage and then deserted. Their families have abandoned them, but at the Magdalen Hospital they find a quiet and safe retreat. They have never been prostitutes and come to the Magdalen to avoid the danger of being forced to such depths. They are carefully examined by a board before admission and are taught Bible reading and household employment. Where possible, they are returned to their families, and since the hospital opened in 1758 more than two-thirds have been forgiven by their families and placed in honest employment, while many of them have married and become respectable members of society again.

Most of these girls are under twenty when they are discharged, and none is allowed to leave without the proper provision for work or a forgiving family.

Near the Westminster Lying-in Hospital, is one established in 1758 for orphans with no relatives able to support them. They are taken in at nine years old and sent off at fourteen into apprenticed trades or domestic service. This hospital is supported by voluntary contributions and Sunday collections at chapel and church doors.

The Marine Society in Bishopsgate, established in 1756, fits out volunteers in time of war to serve as seamen on the King's ships, and at all times admits distressed boys for sea service. The society has provided a ship, large enough to receive a hundred boys, which lies moored between Deptford and Greenwich, and there is a schoolmaster on board as well as naval officers to teach the boys their naval duties.

The Bayswater General Lying-in Hospital, under the patronage of the Queen and supported by voluntary subscriptions, is for the distressed wives of soldiers and sailors, and also cares for penniless infants, some of whom are already orphaned.

There is a School for the Indigent Blind in St George's Fields, where at the present time there are nineteen boys and nine girls. They make baskets and cordage, which are on sale at the school.

In Craven Street, off the Strand, is the Society for the Relief and Discharge of Persons Confined for Small Debts. Established in 1772, within fifteen months it was able to discharge 986 prisoners – mostly seamen and labourers trying to exist on very small wages – who were being imprisoned no longer for the small debt they had incurred but because they were unable to pay the fees imposed on debtors by the prison, from the time of their incarceration.

The humanity of this society brought relief not only to those 986 prisoners but to the wives and children lodging with them.

In Parliament Street there is a Society for Bettering the Condition of the Poor. The Philanthropic Society in St George's Fields was established in 1788, for the rescue of young children, some of whom would have been sold into prostitution by vicious and dishonest parents.

The Humane Society, promoted by Dr Hawes in 1774, has already restored nearly 3,000 patients from apparent death by strangulation and every kind of suffocation. The society's receiving house, fitted with modern apparatus, is in Hyde Park.

The Samaritan Society, attached to the London Hospital, looks after patients who have been discharged as cured but who cannot immediately find work. Established only nine years ago, it has already saved many from a life of beggary or crime. There are seventy life directors, who have given 5 guineas each to establish the society, other members paying an annual subscription of one guinea.

There are numerous public dispensaries throughout London, where it is estimated that some 50,000 poor people are supplied each year with free medicine and advice, while at least a third of them are attended in their own homes. This scheme is only just beginning, under the keen promotion of Dr Lettson.

There are also many workhouses in London nowadays, most of them established during the last twenty-five years, a period in which practical sympathy for the sick and poor has been growing so steadily. Two of the best are the St Marylebone Workhouse, in Paddington New Road, near the upper end of Baker Street, with accommodation for more than a thousand people, and St Martin's Workhouse in Castle Street, Leicester Square.

The Royal Hospital, Chelsea, with lovely gardens running down to the riverside, was established by Charles II in 1682 and is a refuge for some 500 war veterans who are either wounded, disabled or too old to look after themselves and incapable of supplementing their meagre pensions by any work. They must be on the permanent pension list and of good character. They must show that they have rendered good service to the army 'by Flood and Field', and they must not have a wife or children dependent on them.

At the hospital the veterans are fed and clothed and given the best medical attention available. They are provided with long scarlet coats, lined with blue, and the old-fashioned tricorn hat – the uniform which was worn by the Duke of Marlborough's armies

The botanical gardens at Chelsea

a century ago. They are divided into six companies, each company being responsible for the cleaning of its wards and the preservation of order.

The men are given beef on Sundays and mutton on weekdays, apart from one day each week when they have bacon for a change, and they have a daily allowance of a pint of porter.

The Greenwich Hospital for Seamen was established a few years after the hospital at Chelsea: the architect of both was Sir Christopher Wren, and the Greenwich hospital is run on similar lines to the Chelsea hospital.

The Foundling Hospital is today in Lamb's Conduit Fields. It was established by royal charter granted in 1739 to Thomas Coram, the master of a trading vessel, for the reception, maintenance and education of orphaned or abandoned children, the boys to be apprenticed to a trade, the girls to be put to domestic service or apprenticed to dressmakers. Coram was moved to the creation of this hospital because, as he said in his petition for the charter: 'No expedient has been found out for preventing the frequent murders of poor infants at their birth, or for suppressing the custom of exposing them to perish in the streets, or putting them out to nurses who, undertaking to bring them up for small sums, suffered

Children at play at the Foundling Hospital

them to starve, or, if permitted to live, either turned them out to beg or steal, or hired them out to persons, by whom they are trained up in that way of living and sometimes blinded or maimed, in order to move pity, and thereby become fitter instruments of gain to their employers.'

The first hospital was a house in Hatton Garden, opened in 1740. People were invited to bring unwanted babies there, and it was expressly stated that no questions would be asked concerning the child's identity. The house had room for only twenty children, although many more were brought there, and by 1754 the present hospital had been built in Lamb's Conduit Fields – within a few months 600 children had been admitted. Still no questions were asked, and on arrival the babies were placed in a basket hung at the gates of the hospital.

When the hospital extended its work to include babies outside London, they began to arrive from all parts of the country, with no indication of their identity, brought to the hospital by a carrier, who was paid in advance. An unscrupulous carrier, having already been paid, would sometimes abandon the baby. Some were mercilessly drowned, others shamefully neglected. It was reported in the House of Commons that one carrier, bringing five babies to the

182

hospital, lay down on a common and fell into a drunken sleep all night, and when he awoke he found that three of the five babies were dead. Sometimes the baby's clothing was stolen and the baby delivered into the hospital basket wearing nothing at all.

After four years, 15,000 babies had been deposited in the hospital basket but only 4,400 of them survived. The Government, realizing that this easy way of getting rid of an unwanted child and the indiscriminate manner of admission were encouraging profligacy, withdrew their grant of £500,000.

The hospital governors then decided that the only way they could carry on was to announce that a £100 note must accompany every child left in the basket, and still no questions would be asked. As only the wealthy can leave children there on those terms, it means that profligacy is being encouraged amongst the prosperous classes, but that is the system which pertains today, although it is so scandalous that strong protests are already being made.

When Sophie v. la Roche visited the hospital a few years ago, she noted that,

> The girls were playing all kinds of games on one side of the large lawns, the boys on the other; they looked bright and attractive and very healthy. Approximately ten boys were harnessed to a roller, which they were lustily trailing across the sand so as to level it. Their brown clothes bound with red, and the girls' white pinafores made a pleasant sight. . . .
>
> The elder girls had laid the tables in very pretty spacious dining-rooms; everything was white and spotless; other girls did the waiting; the meal only consisted of one course of mutton boiled with barley, but it is so well prepared, and served in such quantities, that with their good bread and mug of beer besides, the children could not want anything better.
>
> We were also shown over the bedrooms, where the beds were so cleanly, the air so pure, and everything looked so nice, that I fancied they were symbols of the nation's best characteristics.

Despite its early troubles, the hospital is now receiving generous donations which may help to re-establish itself as Thomas Coram first conceived it.

10. Administration of the Law: Crime and Punishment

Today London's upper crust of gentry, wits and gallants, professional people and wealthy tradesmen is thin, and below them teem the increasing masses of the poor, many of them unemployed and at least a quarter of them destitute paupers, illiterate and helpless. In the filth and obscure squalor of the London slums, they starve, freeze and rot, resorting to crime through the sheer will to keep alive.

The Poor Law of 1601 is still in operation, but its administration is corrupt, and even those who are fortunate enough to receive any benefit find that the money is barely enough to keep them alive.

For wrongdoers the penalties are harsh, but desperation usually drives them to take the risks involved. As late as 1769 there were 160 offences listed for which the penalty was death or transportation. They included murder, treason, coining false money, arson, rape, sodomy, piracy, forgery, burglary, highway robbery, house-breaking, picking pockets above a shilling, shoplifting above 5 shillings, stealing above forty shillings from any house, setting fire to corn or coal mines, taking reward for helping another to conceal stolen goods, returning from transportation, sending threatening letters, concealing the death of a bastard child, stealing horses, cattle or sheep, breaking prison and robbery of the mail.

There are records of men and women being hanged for stealing no more than 5 shillings, while for minor offences the penalties are fines (for those who have money to pay them), the pillory or the stocks. Yet with no proper organization to control or apprehend them, many have escaped justice, and the less stout-hearted among the poor are too frightened or too anxious for a possible share of the loot to help the cause of the law.

It was not until eight years ago that stipendiary magistrates, with regular incomes, were appointed in England. Before then, justice was administered as it had been since medieval times, by unpaid Justices of the Peace chosen by the Lords Lieutenant of the counties to govern their districts for the Crown. They administered either at the quarter and petty sessions or from their own homes, and their duties included the levying of the county rate, the maintenance of roads and bridges, the licensing of taverns, the administration of the Poor Law, and the supervision of houses of correction, prisons and workhouses. Constables whose task it was to help the magistrates and maintain law and order were also unpaid citizens, and they took yearly office.

In country districts, men of integrity can usually be found to fill the newly created posts of stipendiary magistrates, but in London it is a different story, for the punishments they have the power to inflict are severe, and prisoners with means at their disposal are only too thankful when they find anyone prepared to accept a bribe which will save them from a prison sentence.

Since 1792, therefore, men of 'lesser calibre' – whom the Scottish novelist Tobias Smollett has described as 'of profligate lives, needy, mean, ignorant and rapacious' – have sometimes bribed their way into being appointed Justices of the Peace, in order to make a living out of the public by extortion and corrupt use of their powers. These 'trading justices' did well for themselves, for the penalties they enforced, were heavy enough to warrant the greatest possible financial sacrifice on the part of the prisoners and their friends.

Eight years ago the system of the trading justices who received no salary but made their incomes from fines they imposed on delinquents was abolished. Magistrates may impose fines but not receive them, and the money is paid into Court.

In London, the system of voluntary constables has long since broken down. People took to delegating their duties, for a small payment, to men prepared to do the work for them. As early as Charles II's time these watchmen, known as 'Charlies', had become a recognized institution, though they were, for the most part, far too old for the work and hopelessly ineffective. 'They were chosen out of those poor, old, decrepit people who are from their want of bodily strength rendered incapable of getting a living by work,' wrote Henry Fielding. 'These men, armed only with a pole, which some of them are scarce able to lift, are to secure the persons and houses of His Majesty's subjects from the attacks of young, bold, stout and desperate well-armed villains . . . if the poor old fellows should run away from such enemies no one, I think, can wonder unless he should wonder that they are able even to make their escape.'

This past century, as the population of London has increased from half a million people to close on a million, so has the crime rate, and with no police force to keep proper watch, the criminals are often never brought to justice. As a result, the power and unruly condition of London artisans was becoming dangerous and intolerable by the middle of the century. There were riots during elections, strikes for higher wages, and street fighting all day long and every day.

From time to time there were 'Presentments' by the Grand Jury of Middlesex for the maintenance of religion and order and the discouragement of vice. In 1728 the Grand Jury pointed out the evils resulting from gin drinking, the increase of beggars and the immoralities of the masquerades, and after this it was made illegal to sell spirits in a quantity less than two gallons without a licence. In 1741 there was a protest against the interference of soldiers during an election and a still greater increase in the number of beggars, while in 1744 the complaint was of increased luxury and extravagance, and the existence of gaming houses.

By 1731 a pamphlet was published decrying the increase of violence and robberies in the City of London:

Violence and plunder are no longer confined to the highways, where the robbers have lurking-places to hide, and numberless turnings to avoid and escape the pursuit of the country. . . . The scene is quite changed, the field of action is remov'd; and the actors themselves are likewise changed; the streets of the City are now the places of danger; men are knock'd down and robb'd, nay, sometimes murdered at their own doors, and in passing and repassing from house to house, or from shop to shop.

Stage coaches are robbed in High Holborn, Whitechapel, Pall Mall, Soho, and at almost all the avenues to the City. Hackney coaches and gentlemen's coaches are stopt in Cheapside, St Paul's Churchyard, the Strand and other the most crowded streets, and that even while the people in throngs are passing and repassing, as it were at their elbows.

Nor are these personal violences the only grievances which we have to complain of; but the boldness and multitude of lewd and disorderly persons of both sexes, which throng the streets as soon as the evening may be said to begin, are such, that renders it not only unpleasant, but indeed unsafe, to honest and modest people to be abroad, or go from place to place, however lawful or however urgent their occasions may be.

Another sinister practice involved sending threatening letters to householders, demanding that they leave money at a particular place or their houses would be set on fire, or they and their families murdered.

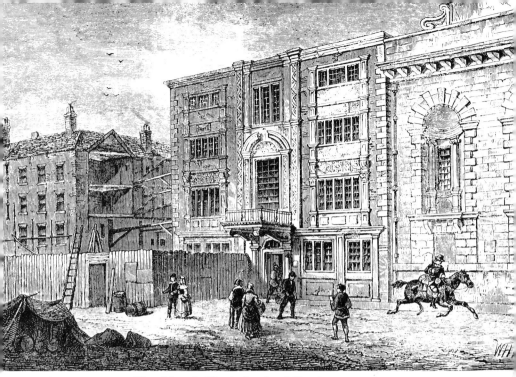

The old post office in Lombard Street

The writer of the pamphlet exposes the fact that the watchmen and constables are often in league with the robbers and are bribed by them to turn a blind eye to their misdeeds.

After Rich opened the Covent Garden Theatre in 1732, although one or two of the taverns frequented by the actors remained orderly, the surrounding courts and alleys – Helmet Court, Edge Court, Windsor Court, Russell Court and Vinegar Yard, with the Star tavern – became murky and evil, the abode of thieves, prostitutes and unsuccessful authors, some of whom were employed by Curll, the publisher of obscene literature, to write salacious pieces for him.

The highwayman Dick Turpin began his career of crime as a footpad in the narrow, unlit streets of London. Covent Garden was infested with them, and the poet William Shenstone, writing fifty years ago, said: 'London is really dangerous at this time; the pickpockets, formerly contented with mere filching, make no scruple to knock people down with bludgeons in Fleet Street and the Strand, and that at no later hour than eight o'clock at night; but in the Piazzas, Covent Garden, they come in large bodies, armed with couteaus [knives] and attack whole parties, so that the danger of coming out of the playhouses is of some weight in the opposite scale when I am disposed to go to them oftener than I ought.'

187

The Mohawks were a different breed, for they were by no means indigent but bands of disorderly, dissolute young men who took a delight in attacking and alarming passers-by. 'They seldom ventured within the City proper, where the watch was more efficient than in any other part,' writes Peter Cunningham, 'but took their stand about St Clement Danes and Covent Garden, breaking the watchman's lantern and halberd, and frequently locking him up in his own stand-box.' 'They began their evening at their clubs,' writes another observer, 'by drinking to excess in order to inflame what little courage they possessed; they then sallied forth, sword in hand. Some enacted the part of "dancing masters" by thrusting their rapiers between the legs of sober citizens in such a fashion as to make them cut the most grotesque capers . . . another trick was for a pack of Mohawks to surround their victim and form a circle with the points of their swords. One gave him a puncture in the rear, which very naturally made him wheel about; then came a prick from another; and so they kept him spinning like a top till in their mercy they chose to let him go free.' Sometimes they would merely swagger about the town, amusing themselves by 'breaking windows, upsetting sedans, beating quiet men, and offering rude caresses to pretty women'.

Professional crime continues unabated. Plunder is easy to sell, for there are pawnbrokers willing to buy anything that is brought to them, most of which they send over to Rotterdam or Antwerp, where they sell it at a satisfactory profit.

Criminals usually work together, meeting at a favourite tavern in order to make their plans – there are today 5,204 taverns in London, one for every 200 people. Coiners of base money come to their taverns to sell and exchange their coin. Card-sharpers bring their victims here, apprentices the property they have stolen from their masters. The old iron and rag shops also receive stolen goods. Patrick Colquhoun, a police magistrate, estimated that there were 3,000 of these shops in London, handling each year more than £700,000 worth of property from petty thefts.

Theft from ships moored in the Thames has been estimated at £500,000 a year, and there are also serious thefts from the storehouses alongside the river, when, for example, clerks and storekeepers report stocks as unserviceable. Colquhoun, in his report on this scandal, said, 'It would scarcely be credited to what an enormous extent the sale of cheap cordage, sail-cloth and other naval articles is carried, in supplying coasting vessels and smaller craft upon the river Thames, which has been plundered in a variety of ways.'

Thieving Lane

The trade of false coinage is also flourishing and there are known to be between forty and fifty mints working secretly in London, one coiner having admitted counterfeiting £200,000 worth of half-crowns.

The total loss from ordinary robberies, river robberies, dockyard robberies and false coinage is estimated at £2 million a year, and the amount of money paid out in rewards at £7,770.

In 1748 the novelist and playwright Henry Fielding was appointed magistrate for Westminster and Middlesex and given a house in Bow Street, with a salary of £300 a year, 'of the dirtiest money upon earth'. His half-brother John, who as a youth had been blinded in an accident, was appointed his assistant.

The Government asked Henry Fielding to submit a plan to combat the alarmingly rising crime rate. In 1751 he published his

Enquiry into the Causes of the late increase of Robbers, etc, with some Proposals for Remedying the Growing Evil, and he formulated the plan for a new police force, the Bow Street Runners, but only three years later he died, and it was John who took over the task of curbing professional crime and establishing methods of administration of criminal justice. Known as 'the Blind Beak', he was said to be able to recognize some 3,000 thieves just by their voices.

At first there were only six Bow Street Runners, but they were men of special skill in solving crimes and were prepared to travel anywhere in the country, or even abroad, where their help was needed. In addition to this 'special branch', John Fielding had a patrol of sixty-eight men based on the Bow Street office. They were divided into thirteen parties, each comprising an officer and three or four men, and they patrolled the streets at night and at other

Milford Lane

times when there were large gatherings which might break out into disorder. The Runners were armed with cutlasses, and the officers also carried a brace of pistols. There were never more than twelve Bow Street Runners, and usually there were only eight. They did not wear a special uniform, and one of them, Townshend, who often used to guard the King, when he was Prince of Wales, was well known for his wide-brimmed hat and flamboyant clothes, his insignia of office being a small baton surmounted by a crown.

A citizen now leaves the apprehension of a criminal to a thief-taker, for any attempt to arrest the robber himself, which he has every right to do, inevitably results in an armed assault by the criminal's confederates. A person who has been robbed sometimes advertises for the return of his property, offering a reward and the promise 'no questions asked', which again is an invitation to the dishonest thief-taker.

Constables themselves are now turned into thief-takers and are given rewards for the apprehension and prosecution of offenders. Some thief-takers associate with the criminals, promise – for a fee – not to report them and then, when the crime has been committed, report the guilty men and receive the informers' reward.

Although the system of rewards for informing on criminals is still in force, it is now under review, and there are also plans to set up new police courts in London, at Queen Square, Great Marlborough Street, Hatton Garden, Worship Street, Lambeth Street, Whitechapel, High Street, Shadwell, and Main Street, Southwark.

William Wilberforce, who is agitating for the emancipation of the slaves, is also deeply concerned by the increasing violent crime in London during recent years. In 1784, when he was still in his twenties, he was converted to the Evangelical Christianity of the Wesleys and George Whitfield, and that year helped to set up the Society for the Reformation of Manners, which was designed to raise the moral standards of Englishmen. He and his friends were originally known as 'The Saints', but since his marriage three years ago, when he went to live at Clapham, they have been known as 'the Clapham Sect'. His next publication was *A Practical View of the Prevailing Religious System of Professed Christianity in the Higher and Middle Classes of the Country Contrasted with Real Christianity*.

There is no doubt that the Clapham Sect have had a good influence on certain sections of society. They have brought about the royal proclamation which has been read from every pulpit in the country and promoted a crusade to raise the standard of morals and manners. The Vice Society has been set up to enforce the

View of Clapham in 1790

King's proclamation, and within the last twelve months its members, together with informers whom they have paid to spy on their neighbours, have brought to court 678 offenders, often under the terms of some long-forgotten law which has remained on the statute book. One of the vices condemned in the proclamation was profanation of the Sabbath, and 623 people have been convicted and fined in London and a further 3,000 warned.

Perhaps debt is no more a real crime than Sabbath-breaking, but once a man or woman is committed to a debtors' prison, life becomes very hard. Those with any money at all have to pay for their lodging. Living conditions are appalling, and food comprises only basics, prisoners being expected to provide anything better themselves, usually by bribing the gaolers to buy it for them. Once committed, debtors remain in prison until their debts are paid, and if there is no one to help them, they remain there for the rest of their lives, which are usually cut short by starvation and disease.

Criminals whose misdemeanours have been committed in London or the county of Middlesex are tried at the Old Bailey. There are eight sessions a year, at which one of twelve judges presides. Trial is by jury but, although there is a counsel for the prosecution, no counsel is allowed for the defence.

It sometimes happens that the offence a prisoner has committed carries such a heavy penalty, under an old decree that has never been rescinded, that neither the jury nor the magistrate will convict. This is the record of the fate of prisoners tried in the year from April 1793 to March 1794 at the London Sessions, which include Middlesex and Westminster:

Persons committed for trial	1,660
Acquitted and discharged	567
Condemned to death	68
Transportation for 14 years	2
Transportation for 7 years	167
Whipped and imprisoned	48
Imprisoned for 6 months or more	80
Imprisoned for 3 months	69
Sent to join the army	38
Judgement delayed	21

When John Howard visited some of the London prisons twenty-five years ago, he was appalled at the squalor and misery he found and devoted the following years, until his death ten years ago, to trying to improve matters.

He found that gaolers and their assistants were unpaid, depending on fees from the prisoners for their own subsistence, and he found men who had been declared innocent, and others whose prosecutors had not appeared, still detained for months, until they had found the money to pay their gaol delivery fees. Now there is no longer any payment imposed on those found not guilty, to impede their release.

There has been a prison at Newgate, the fifth main gate of the City wall, for at least 500 years. Although the original building, already condemned, was burnt down twenty years ago, during the Gordon Riots, it was at once rebuilt on the same plan. In 1754 Strype wrote:

It is a large prison and made very strong, the better to secure such sort of criminals, which too much fill it. It is a dismal place within. The prisoners are sometimes packed so close together, and the air so corrupted by their stench and nastiness, that it occasions a disease called the Jail distemper, of which they die by dozens, and cartloads of them are carried out and thrown into a pit in the churchyard of Christ's Church, without ceremony; and so infectious is this distemper, that several judges, jurymen, and lawyers, have taken it off the prisoners, when they have been brought to the Old Bailey to be tried, and died soon after . . . of which we have an instance within these seven years. And to this wretched place, innocent people are sometimes sent, and loaded with irons before their trial, not to secure them, but to extort money from them by a merciless jailer; for if they have money to bribe him, they may have the irons as light as they please. The City have been so good lately as to introduce a ventilator on the top of Newgate, to expel the foul air and to introduce fresh, to preserve the prisoners' health, and the prisoners are many of them kept in distant and more airy prisons, till within a few days of their trials. Sweet herbs, also, are strewed in the court and the passages of it, to prevent infection; and the snuffing up vinegar, it is said, is the most likely way to preserve the health of those that are obliged to attend such trials.

When Sir John Howard visited the prison in 1779, he wrote that the cells for condemned malefactors, built in old Newgate after the great fire of 1666, were still used for the same purpose: 'In the upper part of each cell is a window, double grated, near 3 feet by 1½. The doors are four inches thick. The strong stone wall is lined all round each cell with planks, studded with broad-headed nails. In each cell is a barrack bedstead. I was told by those that attended them that criminals who had affected an air of boldness during their trial, and appeared quite unconcerned at the pronouncing sentence upon them, were struck with horror, and shed tears, when brought to these darksome, solitary abodes.'

When Howard visited the prison shortly after the second re-building, he said: 'The men's quadrangle is now divided into three courts. In the first court are those who pay 3s.6d a week for a bed; in the next, the poorer felons; and in the other *now*, the women. Under the chapel are cells for the refractory. Two rooms, adjoining the condemned cells, are built for an infirmary, in one of which, at my last visit, there were sixteen sick.'

As for food, from various charities which have been granted to the prison, every Saturday debtors are given eight stone of beef to share, and in some years felons also receive this. Prisoners retained while they pay their fines have four stone of beef every Saturday. There are also bequests which supply them with a certain amount of bread. Other food they buy from the warder if they have any money.

Of the 291 prisoners Howard found in Newgate in 1782, 225 were men and sixty-six women. Nearly a hundred of them were in transit to the hulks, prison ships anchored offshore, for transportation to New South Wales and Norfolk Island had not yet begun;

eighty-nine were fines; twenty-one were under sentence of death, and the remainder lay for trial. Some of the condemned had 'been long sick and languishing in their cells'.

Howard found that the practice of paying fees to the gaoler still persisted, despite the fact that through his protest to the Government the gaoler was receiving a salary and no longer dependent on the prisoners for his livelihood. On leaving prison, debtors and felons still had to pay 8s.10d, those committed for misdemeanours and those condemned to transportation 14s.10d.

The King's Bench Prison for debtors is in Southwark, at the

The condemned cell in Newgate Prison

entrance to the Borough Road. Colonel John Hanger, who was released from there only last year, after a stay of ten months, said that, 'It rivals the purlieus of Wapping, St Giles and St James's in vice, debauchery and drunkenness.' The immorality he found there was so great '. . . that it was almost impossible to escape contagion'. He determined to consort, if he could, only with the few who remained gentlemen of honour, lest he lose 'every sense of honour and dignity; every moral principle and virtuous disposition'.

As for the women prisoners, he said, 'No unhappy and unfortunate female ever did, nor do I believe ever will, quit this seat of contamination without the most degrading, if not fatal, effects of such a situation.'

The prisoners in the King's Bench vary in number from 350 to 500 and, 'There are seldom fifty who have any regular means of subsistence. . . . They do not starve but are underfed, often subsisting on only one meal in two days and without a penny for a roll of bread for breakfast.' Those with no money at all are entitled to 6d a day from their creditor, but all too often this is withheld. The debtor can obtain it by demand at Westminster Hall, but this entails expense far beyond its value – the fee for the tipstaff who goes with the prisoner being 10 shillings, the fee for being at liberty to leave the prison under supervision for a day 4 shillings, the fee for the attorney attending at the King's Bench 6s.8d, and for attending at Westminster another 6s.8d.

Hanger, writing this year, sums up:

It is not possible for me at present to speak with certainty to the fact, not having as yet obtained an account of the number of prisoners who are confined in the various prisons of London for debts under £10. But I call God to witness that from the conversations I have held with various prisoners in the King's Bench (in the Fleet it is exactly the same), and the information I have acquired on the subject, I truly believe that I speak much within the compass, when I with horror inform you that above one-half of the prisoners in the King's Bench and the Fleet (aye, in most of the other jails in England), could be liberated, and would be liberated to-morrow, were it not for the costs that must be paid to the attorney before they can be discharged.

The rent of a bed and bedding at the King's Bench is 3d a night or 1s.9d a week, unless the prisoner brings his own bed, when he is charged a shilling a week for a place to put it. If he cannot afford this, he either shares a bed or sleeps on the floor.

The King's Bench Prison for Debtors at Southwark

On arrival he pays fees to the marshal, the turnkey, the tipstaff who brings him from the court and various other officers, a sum which amounts to £6.2s. – and he has to pay nearly as much again when he leaves.

The 'rules' – the bounds of the prison – are fairly extensive, with a circumference of about three miles, and here prisoners may live and earn money by following their craft. There are also 'day rules', which means the prisoners can work outside the prison during the daytime but must return each night.

The Fleet Prison at the bottom of Ludgate Hill, overlooking the Fleet ditch, has for the last 150 years been reserved mainly for debtors. Like Newgate, it was burned down during the Great Fire of 1666, rebuilt, destroyed during the Gordon Riots but rebuilt at once on its former plan.

When John Howard visited it twenty-four years ago, he said it was an ill-managed prison:

> The prisoners play in the courtyard at skittles, mississippi, fives, tennis etc. And not only the prisoners. I saw among them several butchers and others from the market, who are admitted here, as at another public-house. The same may be seen in many other prisons where the gaoler keeps or lets the taps. . . . On Monday night there was a wine club; on Thursday night a beer club; each lasting usually till one or two

197

in the morning. I need not say how much riot these occasion, and how the sober prisoners, and those that are sick, are annoyed by them. . . . Seeing the prison crowded with women and children, I procured an accurate list of them, and found that on (or about) the 6th April, 1776, there were on the Master's Side, 213 prisoners, on the Common Side, 30, total 243; their wives and children were 175.

Describing the newly built prison in 1782, he said:

At the front is a narrow court. At each end of the building there is a small projection or wing. There are four floors – they call them galleries – besides the cellar floor, called 'Bartholomew Fair'. Each gallery consists of a passage in the middle the whole length of the prison, 66 yards; and rooms on each side of it about 14½ feet by 12½, and 9½ feet high; a chimney and window in every room. The passages are narrow (not 7 feet wide) and darkish, having only a window at each end. On the first floor, the hall gallery, to which you ascend by eight steps, are a chapel, a tap-room, a coffee room, a room for the turnkey, another for the watchman, and eighteen rooms for prisoners. Besides the coffee-room and tap-room, two of these eighteen rooms and all the cellar-floor, except a lock-up room to confine the disorderly, and another room for the turnkey, were held by the tapster, John Cartwright, who bought the remainder of the lease at public auction in 1775.

The cellar floor is sixteen steps below the hall-gallery. It consists of the two rooms just now mentioned, the tapster's kitchen, his four large beer and wine cellars, and fifteen rooms for prisoners. These fifteen, and the two before mentioned on the hall-gallery, the tapster lets to prisoners, for from 4/– to 8/– a week. On the second floor . . . are twenty-five rooms for prisoners; on the next gallery, twenty-seven. One of them, fronting the staircase, is their committee room. A room at one end is an infirmary; at the other end, in a large room over the chapel, is a dirty billiard-table, kept by the prisoner who sleeps in that room. On the highest storey are twenty-seven rooms. . . . All the rooms I have mentioned are for Master's Side debtors. The weekly rent of those not held by the tapster is 1/3d unfurnished. . . .

The apartments for Common Side debtors are only part of the right wing of the prison. Besides the cellar (which was intended for their kitchen, but is occupied with lumber and shut up) there are four floors. On each floor is a room about twenty-four or twenty-five feet square, with a fireplace; and on the sides, seven closets or cabins to sleep in. Such of these prisoners as swear in court, or before a commissioner, that they are not worth £5, and cannot subsist without charity, have the donations which are sent in to the prison, the begging box and the grate. Of them there were at my first visit, sixteen, at other times not so many.

The racket court in the Fleet Prison

Before 1753 neither banns nor a licence was necessary for a legal marriage, provided the ceremony was conducted by a man in Holy Orders, and many 'Fleet marriages' were solemnized here by clerics who were prisoners for debt, of couples who wished to be married either secretly or very quickly. At first they were held in the Fleet chapel, but then the local tavern-keepers fitted up rooms for them. But in 1753 an Act was passed requiring banns to be read or a proper licence to be obtained for a marriage to be legal, which meant the end of the Fleet marriages.

Earlier in the past century the conditions of the Fleet and the treatment of some of the prisoners was so cruel that in 1726 there was a Parliamentary investigation. Huggins, in charge of the prison, and his lessee Bainbridge were tried for murder. The trial revealed all too clearly the evils of farming out the prisoners, for Bainbridge was proved to be a callous, greedy sadist who tortured many of his prisoners in order to extract money from them. He and Huggins were given only short, inadequate terms of imprisonment, but from that time there has been a gradual reform in the management of the prison, although it has not gone nearly far enough yet to meet the standards of common humanity.

The Poultry Compter for prisoners committed by the Lord Mayor or aldermen

Ludgate Prison is mainly for debtors who are freemen of the City of London. Established in the Lud Gate in the City Wall in the fourteenth century, then, when the City walls were demolished and the Ludgate with it, moved to Bishopsgate Street, its present site is in Giltspur Street, to which it came, to adjoin the prison already there, only six years ago.

The official protector of all the freemen of the City is the Lord Mayor, who is therefore technically the master of the prison, but inevitably he appoints a keeper, who in his turn appoints a deputy-keeper, who buys his position and also pays a yearly rent. He lives on the prisoners, taking their admission fees and bed money.

When Howard visited the prison there was an average of twenty-two 'freemen' prisoners there. The fees on admission are: to the clerk of the compter, 2s.6d, to the sergeant-at-mace, 5 shillings. The prison fees are a shilling on admission and 3d a week during confinement. A discharge costs 5s.4d if there is only one writ, more if there are several. The clerk charges another 3s.8d, the messenger a shilling and the prison 2 shillings.

The City allows the prisoners 140 pounds of beef every week, and each prisoner receives a 2d loaf every other day. The Lord Mayor and sheriffs send coal each year, and Calvert & Company send two barrels of small ale every two weeks. The bequests to the prison for other benefits amount to some £140 a year.

Today the average number of Ludgate prisoners varies between nine and twenty-eight.

The Wood Street Compter and the Poultry Compter are City prisons for people committed or sentenced by the Lord Mayor or the aldermen, each being in the charge of one of the sheriffs.

The Wood Street Compter, for both debtors and felons, used to be a dirty, verminous place housing some seventy debtors and twenty-eight felons, the debtors being kept in only one room, some thirty-three feet by fifteen feet, where they lived, cooked their food and slept on shelves fixed up against the walls, the highest shelves being reached by a ladder. No straw or bedding was allowed, and there was no medical attention until members of the General Dispensary, which was established thirty years ago, began to visit them and give attention where it was needed.

It was only nine years ago that this terrible place was abandoned and the prisoners moved to the new compter in Giltspur Street, where today debtors and felons are joined by both vagrants and disorderly people who are brought in each night from the streets. Today there are about thirty-six debtors imprisoned there, and the

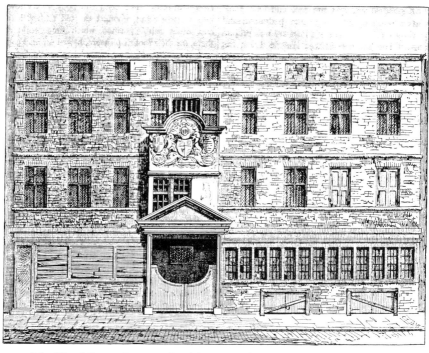

The Wood Street Compter for debtors and felons committed by the Lord Mayor or aldermen

place is a considerable improvement on the old compter, for it has plenty of water available, and the rooms and wards are kept moderately clean.

The Poultry Compter is very old and rapidly falling into decay. It has many small endowments, and the sheriff in charge sends in food from his own table. It contains a separate ward for Jews, and today there are two confined here, both for debt.

There is a tap-room and an infirmary and, as at the Wood Street compter, there is a good supply of water and the place is kept quite clean. There is a communal day room but separate sleeping rooms for the men and women. There are only thirty-three debtors here now, ten of whom have their wives living with them, some of them also bringing their children.

The building is now in such a dangerous condition that in many places it is shored up with props. Plans are now afoot for transferring the debtors to Giltspur Street, while the old place is repaired.

The New Prison, Clerkenwell is another dreary place, although it was rebuilt in 1775. The night rooms are furnished with barrack beds. The day rooms for the men and women are separate – both being long, low sheds. The number of prisoners here varies between fifty and ninety.

Whitechapel Prison is a debtors' prison for Stepney and Hackney, for people whose debts are over £2 and under £5. There are usually about twenty-five of them, and they hang out a begging box in front of the house, but no one may share the few pence it brings in unless he has paid the keeper's fee of half a crown. In 1782 an Act of Parliament decreed that no debtor should be confined here for more than a week for every pound of his debt. This means that there is seldom a prisoner left here, but the keeper has a licence to sell alcohol, and men from the outside world now come in, play skittles in the courtyard and treat the place like an ordinary tavern.

In Wellclose Square stand the ruins of a prison which was in fact a public house run by a Swede. In it was a court room for the Tower Hamlets, and the garden of the house was converted into a prison yard. The prison rooms consisted of a small closet, 5½ feet by 3½ feet, used as the day room, with three night rooms above, with not even straw for a bed. The few prisoners who were ever incarcerated here were given an allowance of 2d a day, but none has been here for at least twenty years. There was a similar small prison in St Katherine's Precinct.

The Savoy Prison is in the ruins of the Savoy Palace, which in Tudor times was converted into a hospital; it is a military prison for deserters and military delinquents.

The Marshalsea Prison in Southwark is today the Admiralty gaol for pirates, although felons are also admitted.

The episcopal Clink Prison in Deadman's Place, Bankside, was burnt down during the 1780 riots and has never been replaced.

The Bridewells, or Houses of Correction, are also prisons. The City Bridewell is established in the ruins of the Tudor Bridewell Palace and is a melancholy place for 'idle, vagrant, loose and disorderly persons, and "night walkers", who are there set to hard labour but receive clothes and diet.'

John Howard condemned it. The rooms, he said, were offensive. Remains of the beautiful old palace, including a magnificent carved stairway, still stand, and in stark contrast is the whipping room where recalcitrant prisoners were lashed unmercifully. When Pennant visited the prison recently, he said there was not a single male prisoner in the Bridewell but twenty young girls, the eldest no more than sixteen, 'all clad in the silken tatters of squalid finery' and employed in beating hemp.

The steward received 8d a day for each prisoner, and a help-dresser, paid a salary of £20, received the profit of the prisoners' labours. For bedding, the girls were given fresh straw once a month.

The Bridewell at Tothill Fields, Westminster, has about fifty to sixty debtors and there are also wards for vagrants, for cases of assault and battery and for the punishment of apprentices. It is much cleaner than most prisons and regularly washed, while the patients themselves are also induced to wash. When Howard visited it, he was agreeably surprised and said it was 'remarkably well managed' and that its keeper, George Smith, was 'a model to other governors'.

Six years ago a new Penitentiary House was built at Cold Bath Fields, replacing the original Bridewell there, which was built in the reign of James I, when the City Bridewell was no longer large enough to hold London's vagabonds and criminals. The new prison was built on a plan drawn up by Howard himself, but by the time it was opened he was dead; and sadly all his benevolent labours and pleas for a more humanitarian treatment of the imprisoned seem to have been completely forgotten here, for already it has acquired a reputation for undue severity. Men, women and boys are herded together. They suffer desperately from the tyranny and avarice of the turnkeys, and the governor has just introduced the treadmill.

Conclusion: 1800 – the Dawn of the New Century

So this is London at the dawn of a new century. The King seems to have recovered from the attack of insanity he suffered in 1788, and five years ago the Prince of Wales married his cousin Princess Caroline of Brunswick. Although he was secretly married to Mrs Fitzherbert, the marriage was illegal, for as heir to the throne he was not allowed to marry a Roman Catholic, and under the Royal Marriage Act he should have obtained the consent of the King. However, his marriage to Princess Caroline has proved so unhappy that this year he has deserted her, as well as his mistress, Lady Jersey, and returned to Mrs Fitzherbert for a time. She has just celebrated the occasion by a brilliant reception at her home at Brighthelmstone.

The war with France goes on, and this year Malta surrendered to the British Navy, thereby making Britain mistress of the Mediterranean and foretelling the end of French rule in Egypt. This summer, Admiral Nelson left Naples for London in the company of Sir Ian and Lady (Emma) Hamilton, and it is clear to everyone who knows them that Nelson and Emma are beginning to fall in love.

Most of the young intellectuals who in 1789 felt a sympathy for the French revolutionaries fighting against a tyrannical government, have changed their minds now, as they have seen their behaviour after victory.

Mackintosh, who assists his brother-in-law, Daniel Stuart, the editor of the *Morning Post*, has this year announced: 'I abhor, abjure, and for ever renounce the French Revolution, with its sanguinary history, its abominable principles, and for ever execrable leaders.' Like so many others, he has turned back to the liberal Tory tradition of pre-Revolutionary days.

There are several daily papers published in London, all four-page sheets printed on hand-presses and, now that parliamentary reporting is allowed, more are appearing, the most important being the *Morning Post*, first published in 1772, which became a successful business venture, for like all newspapers it depends on

Wife & no wife or *A trip to the continent*. Left to right *Carlo Khan's
political satire shows: North, Burke, Prince George, Mrs Fitzherbert
and Fox*

advertising. By 1784 its circulation was 2,100 daily and it sold for 3½d a copy. The following year the *Times* appeared and was so popular that the circulation of the *Morning Post* dwindled disastrously to only 350 a day, and the owners sold out to Daniel Stuart for £600. But under Stuart's brilliant editing the *Morning Post* has recovered. Within two years the circulation had risen to 1,000 a day, and now it is approaching 2,000 and is still increasing. Its chief leader writer is Samuel Taylor Coleridge.

Magazines and reviews indicate the state of public opinion on science, literature and general taste, but the reviews remain anonymous and are not accountable for any injury they may do to an author by adverse criticism.

Until ten years ago there was no magazine in London worth considering except Edward Cave's *Gentleman's Magazine*, on which Dr Johnson worked so successfully and which contains abridgements of party pamphlets, critical notes and poetry, short biographical memorials of people of note who have recently died and accounts of important public events. There are a number of inferior imitations of the *Gentleman's Magazine*, but now the successful *Monthly Magazine* has appeared, selling about 6,000 each month, and several more have recently been launched, so that an estimated 50,000 magazines are sold in London each month.

Books are published in weekly or monthly numbers, including dictionaries of arts and sciences. About 700 new books issue from the printing presses each year, as well as new editions of established works. This year 692 books have been published, including novels, biographies, poetry, voyages and travels, serious history, drama, medicine, surgery and science, their total cost being £235.5.0.

There are a number of circulating libraries in London these days, and books in many languages are available. Moreover, some booksellers are specializing in the sale of books no longer in print.

London is the focus of all the literature of the country and there are about 300 full-time professional authors, but of these only about a hundred can be said to live solely by their writing, their total income amounting to £20,000 a year.

At the beginning of a new century, with the manifold scientific discoveries of the last few years, Britain stands on the brink of many changes. Joseph Priestley, the Unitarian minister, has discovered the existence of oxygen, and Henry Cavendish the 'inflammable gas' called hydrogen and, with the help of James Watt, has deduced the chemical composition of both air and water. John Dalton has developed his new system of Chemical Philosophy, declaring that every substance is made of an enormous number of indestructible atoms, of different substances and different weights. The Swedish chemist Berzelius has developed Dalton's work, devising chemical symbols, and the Italian Avogadro has prepared the way for the establishment of approximate atomic weights.

As early as 1746 the Duchess of Bedford, in a letter to the Duke, wrote: 'I supped at the Duchess of Montagu's on Tuesday night, where was Mr Baker of the Royal Society, who electrified: it really is the most extraordinary thing one can imagine.' Priestley devised a machine for producing electricity by friction, and since then two Italian professors have produced an electric current in a battery composed of zinc and copper plates. When this news reached the Royal Society in London, British scientists were soon making their own experimental batteries, and the young Humphrey Davy has managed to produce a 'column of electric light' from a battery.

Newcomen invented the first steam engine in the 1730s but now James Watt has devised a new model, using only a quarter of the fuel that Newcomen's first steam pumping engine needed. Watt's steam engine is now used not only to pump water from the steadily deepening coal mines but also for blowing the blast of air necessary for iron smelting. Writing of a new pumping engine he had just installed, he said: 'The velocity, violence, magnitude and horrible noise of the engine gave universal satisfaction.' They are now trying to fit a steam engine to a boat and make it drive paddle-wheels, but the steam engines are so heavy that they nearly sink the boats, and the experiments are regarded as highly dangerous and impractical. George Stephenson has been trying to create a steam locomotive, but so far his first engine has achieved only four miles an hour and consumes so much coal that horse-drawn trucks are both cheaper and quicker.

Over the years there have been many attempts to design a submarine. During the present war with France, the French Government has been offered yet another design – the *Nautilus*. It has a three-man crew and a watertight hull, some twenty feet long by six feet wide, with a rounded, glass-sided conning tower. The keep is a large tank of water ballast, and the weapon a looped metal spike sticking out of the conning tower, which could be driven under the keel of an enemy ship. A rope attached to the spike is towed away, and then a barrel of gunpowder hauled back to the keel and fired. The French Government was greatly impressed with this device but has finally rejected it as being too barbarous a weapon even for warfare.

Balloons are becoming practical now that they are filled with hydrogen, and the highly dangerous fire-baskets, the hot air from which was used to inflate them, are no longer used. Many people thought that balloons would be used in the present war but, although the French use captive balloons, there seems no further interest in them at the moment.

The Government takes no responsibility for education and, as the population has increased so rapidly, the facilities for free education, which in earlier times were provided by wealthy benefactors, are now quite inadequate. It means that today half the population of London cannot read or write.

Amongst the upper classes, some boys are still taught at home by tutors, but an increasing number are now sent away to the fashionable boys' schools, notably Eton, Harrow, Winchester, Rugby and Westminster. Most of these schools were originally grammar school foundations for the free education of local boys, but as prices have risen and headmasters have found that their statutes allow them to admit a certain number of fee-paying students, to augment their own small salaries, the practice of charging fees has grown. Eton has attracted the nobility for many years and a house system has now been established within the school, so that the boys no longer have to live out in the town, in lodgings. Harrow has also become fashionable and now has far more fee-paying students than free scholars.

Many of these boys move on to Oxford or Cambridge, where the educational standards have sunk to a deplorably low level. Endowments for professorships have diminished in value, and dons are therefore ill-paid. They give very few lectures, and tuition is mainly by individual tutors. However, movements for a drastic reform are under way, and this year, for the first time, a written and oral Bachelor of Arts examination has been established at Oxford – no doubt a similar introduction will soon be made at Cambridge.

After leaving the university, many students make the 'Grand Tour' of France and Italy or move to one of the Inns of Court for a legal training, even if they do not propose to practice.

The grammar schools are in a similar plight to the universities, for their endowments have become so inadequate that they are not properly staffed. Five years ago Lord Chief Justice Kenyon declared that most of the ancient grammar schools had become 'empty without scholars and everything neglected but the receipt of salaries'. In some cases, headmasters pocket the bulk of the money available and employ a half-educated man to do the teaching.

Prime bang up at Hackney. On 12 August 1811, before a crowd of 3,000 gathered to celebrate the Regent's birthday, Sadler ascended from the gardens of the Mermaid Tavern at Hackney

A number of fee-paying day and boarding schools run by private proprietors have come into existence during the last few years, several having opened recently in Hackney, but it is the Dissenters, still barred from the universities, who have made the best contribution to the serious gaps in the facilities for educating young people. Dissenting Academies cater mainly for the middle classes of prosperous traders and merchants and their curricula include science, mathematics and geography, as well as the classics and living languages. Many of these schools are so successful that Anglicans are sending their sons to them, and within the last few years some of the fashionable schools, such as Oundle and Rugby, are copying them.

Middle-class boys and younger sons of small squires are often apprenticed on leaving school to merchants, bankers, apothecaries, attorneys and brewers, paying premiums of anything from £20 to £100 until a few years ago, but recently premiums have risen sharply and today some merchants are asking as much as £1,000 to apprentice a boy.

For the steadily increasing numbers of the working classes, there are still very few chances of any education at all, and most grow up illiterate. There are dame schools for small children, and schools for the older ones, the charge being anything from 4d to 9d a week, but they are run by half-literate men and women who are often looking after a small shop or business at the same time. There are no standards: anyone can open a school and set up as a teacher, one cynic remarking that, 'Their only qualification for this employment being their unfitness for every other.' Yet despite a growing desire for education, there are many people who cannot afford even the few pence that this minimum of learning costs.

The Society for the Propagation of the Gospel runs a few charity schools, their aim being 'to combat Popery and to teach the children of the poor to keep their stations'. By 1714 there were 5,000 children attending these charity schools in London. They were clothed and afterwards apprenticed to a trade. Since then the Charity movement has spread, and both Dissenters and the Church of England have opened schools where reading, writing and arithmetic are taught, with spinning and knitting for the girls.

The general attitude towards the education of girls is, however, that on the whole they get on better without it. Amongst the wealthy, they are taught at home by governesses, learning to read and write, to sew and cook. Sometimes they learn a little French and Italian and to play the spinet or piano. Marriages amongst the wealthy are usually a business arrangement, and parents argue

The Cloisters, Christ's Hospital in 1804. The school was established in the Grey Friars convent near Newgate in 1553

that prospective husbands distrust and dislike educated and intellectual women, while men themselves say that if a woman is educated she will not be amenable and obedient.

There have been many protests and some notable rebels to this attitude in recent years, notably in the 'Blue Stocking' circle which gathered round Mrs Montagu, who died only a few weeks ago. However, the accomplishments of these few outstanding women who, in the main, have educated themselves, have not influenced the general attitude towards the education of women to any great extent. When, a few years ago, Mary Wollstonecraft published her *Vindication of the Rights of Woman*, soon after her *Rights of Man* appeared, most people were horrified, and even the good Hannah More called her a 'disgusting and unnatural character'.

There are no schools for girls to compare with the public schools for boys, or the best of their grammar schools, but boarding schools have now become fashionable, where they are taught the usual French and English, arithmetic and geography, needlework and dancing. The most exclusive in London is in Queen Square, Bloomsbury, which today, under the administration of the highly intelligent Mrs Devis, is known as 'The Young Ladies' Eton' The girls here, in addition to the usual lessons, are trained in manners and decorum – how to enter and leave a room, how to sit and how to rise. At the back of the school a coach is kept where girls can practise ascending and descending from it 'with calmness and grace and without any unnecessary display of ankles'.

There are more than 200 pupils at this school, and the fees are more than 100 guineas a year, but in the teaching of anything except the social graces it offers nothing new.

The Industrial Revolution was dawning but had not yet affected the appearance of the City, while the trade boom which came with the development of power-driven machinery was still on the horizon. When Pastor Morits visited London in 1782 he said that he caught his first view of London from Greenwich, and 'enveloped in thick smoke or fog, St Paul's rose, like some huge mountain, above the enormous mass of buildings'. 'There was hardly less stir and bustle on the river than in some of London's crowded streets', he added, 'with the great ships below the Bridge and the countless swarms of little boats passing and repassing, many with one mast and one sail, and many with none, in which persons of all ranks were passed over.'

He admired the English cleanliness, as other foreign visitors had done. 'The English are certainly distinguished for cleanliness, rich

A Naturel [sic] Genius

and poor', he said, and again: 'no people are so cleanly as the English; nor so particular about neat and clean linen.' But on his way home, waiting by the docks for a favourable wind for Hamburg, he saw the seamier side of London, for he described his sordid little lodging-house as 'one of the most execrable holes in all this great City.'

Vast sums were needed for the development of the Empire and they were provided by the City of London. The City financed the fleets of ships, the great merchant vessels, still under sail then, but soon to be under steam. London also provides the commodity markets. Within the Empire, trade and money exchange freely. London capital invested in Australia, South Africa and Canada brings more profits and business to London, the heart of the Empire. The City is also beginning to lend to other countries outside the Empire, for commercial development, and British sterling is becoming the currency with which the nations of the world do their overseas business.

The initial capital needed to develop the inventions of Arkwright and Hargreaves, Samuel Crompton, Cartwright and James Watt, which have provided the cotton mills of Lancashire and the woollen mills of Bradford and Leeds with power-driven machinery all came from the money market of London.

In 1815 the first steamboat was seen in the Mersey. By 1823 the General Steam Navigation Company of Britain had fifteen small steamers plying between London and Europe. Then Stephenson produced the Rocket, which reached a speed of 35 miles an hour and the railway age was launched, the London and Birmingham railway opening in 1838.

As transport improved and more space was needed in the square mile of the City for offices, people who had formerly lived over their businesses began to move to the suburbs and the old dwelling-houses slowly disappeared. By 1800 Chelsea was no longer a village but a small country town of 12,000, and thirty years later the population had more than trebled. The small, exclusive country town of Kensington was also changing and many more streets and squares were being built. There was a rapid increase of house-building in Highgate, where in 1800 there were less than 300 houses. Hampstead developed as quickly, but Maida Vale and St John's Wood were to remain woodland and open country for several more years. South of the river there was still more building.

At the same time, through new discoveries in medicine and surgery and improved social hygiene, which has reduced the occurrence of infectious diseases, the death rate dropped and the population began to increase rapidly. In 1750 the London death rate was 1:20 but by 1821 it had fallen to 1:40.

It is through the money London is able to provide that Britain, which until now has been predominantly an agricultural country, self-sufficient in essential commodities, is becoming a great manufacturing centre – the workshop of the world, the markets for her goods being assured by the growing needs of the pioneers of her Empire.

Books Consulted

Besant, Sir Walter, *London in the Eighteenth Century* (Adam & Charles Black, 1902)

Borer, Mary Cathcart, *Two Villages – The Story of Chelsea and Kensington* (W. H. Allen, 1973)

——*The Years of Grandeur – The Story of Mayfair* (W. H. Allen, 1975)

——*The City of London* (Constable, 1977)

Boswell, James, *The Life of Samuel Johnson* (1791)

Chancellor, E. B., *The Eighteenth Century in London* (Batsford, 1950)

Hindle, Wilfrid, *The Morning Post* (Routledge, 1937)

v. la Roche, Sophie, *Sophie in London* – a diary, August to December 1786, translated from the German by Clare Williams (Jonathan Cape, 1933)

Phillips, Richard, *Modern London – Being the History and Present State of the British Metropolis* (1804)

Stonestreet, George Griffin, *Reflections on Domestic Union – or London as it Should Be* (1800)

Old and New London, Volumes I–VI (Cassell and Co. 1888–93)

Index